Double Over

Alphonse Allais

Double Over

Blackcattish Stories

Translated and with an introduction, notes,
& illustrations by Doug Skinner

2016

DOUBLE OVER:
Blackcattish Stories

by Alphonse Allais

Translated from the French by Doug Skinner

Cover & book design by Norman Conquest

ACKNOWLEDGEMENTS:

This collection was originally published by Ollendorff in France in 1891 under the title *À se tordre: Histoires chatnoiresques.*

ISBN-13 978-0-997-77713-0

FIRST AMERICAN EDITION
November, 2016

Black Scat Books
E-mail: **blackscat@outlook.com**
Web: **BlackScatBooks.com**

Dedicated posthumously to Rodolphe Salis,
proprietor of the Chat Noir, for helping to
uphold the standards of pharmacy.

Contents

—EXTRA STORIES—

Alphonse Allais's Apprenticeship

We should probably feel sorry for Charles-Auguste and Alphonsine Allais. A perfectly respectable couple in the Norman town of Honfleur, they conscientiously filled their neighbors' prescriptions in their pharmacy on la place de la Grande-Fontaine. They had five children; one died shortly after birth, leaving Jeanne, Paul-Émile, and Marguerite. And Charles-Alphonse, born on October 20, 1854, at three in the afternoon—two hours, as has been noted, before Rimbaud popped out in Charleville.

As a child, Alfi (or Fifi, as he was sometimes called) showed little promise. As soon as he could walk, he pissed in the closets. It took him until the age of three to start talking. Despite his later reputation as a prankster, he wasn't a mischievous child. Instead, as his sister Jeanne recalled: "Lazy and absent-minded, he was, in general, considered a mediocre student... If he wasn't a diligent pupil, he was at least a peaceful one, never causing trouble in class, except for occasional outbursts of hilarity at his answers, which were appreciated more by his friends than by his teachers." He did rally, however, receiving good grades and several prizes. French, Latin, Greek, chemistry, and math were his strong points, history and geography were not.

By the time he was eighteen, he had apparently developed into an intelligent and presentable future pharmacist, ready for his formal training in Paris. M. and Mme Allais had every reason to expect that he would diligently serve his apprenticeship, and then return to Honfleur to work in the family business.

Being intelligent, however, Alphonse soon learned that cabarets, cafes, and theaters were more fun than the École de Pharmacie, and that the Bohemian life of Montmartre offered livelier companions and much livelier girlfriends.

The promising pharmaceutical career evaporated in the usual tumult of poetry, plays, absinthe, and cocottes. He became popular, admired for his blonde elegance, his deadpan reserve, his wild imagination, and his penchant for elaborate pranks. His background in chemistry gave him an intriguing scientific reputation, which he maintained with experiments in color photography, synthetic gems, instant coffee, and artificial rubber, often with his brother Paul or with the poet and inventor Charles Cros.

He wrote jokes and short articles for many little papers, including *Le Tintamarre*, *L'Hydropathe*, and *L'Anti-Concierge*. Like his friends, he too submitted burlesque artworks to the Incoherents' Exhibits and wrote monologues for the actor Coquelin Cadet.

In 1881, Rodolphe Salis opened his cabaret, Le Chat

Noir, and Allais soon established himself as a regular. Five years later, Allais became the editor of its house weekly, a spirited little sheet of humor and literature.

In *Le Chat Noir*, Allais ended up serving another kind of apprenticeship: in journalism. He contributed articles, short stories (not always humorous), reviews, and verses, and learned to meet deadlines (usually at the last minute, but still). He became adept at spinning a one-liner into a page and at producing amusing copy when he had nothing to say. He famously took on the conservative theater critic Francisque Sarcey, not only mimicking Sarcey's smug and rambling style, but appropriating his byline. This, naturally, caused somewhat of a scandal, which only meant more publicity for the paper.

Four of his monologues for Cadet were published by the Parisian company Ollendorff, in 1887, 1888, 1889, and 1890. The next year, Ollendorff brought out his first collection, *À se tordre*, subtitled *Histoires chatnoiresques*.

For *À se tordre*, whose first English translation you now grip so reverently, Allais chose the stories he wanted to preserve from his stint at the *Chat Noir*. As the subtitle indicates, it was meant to evoke the ambiance and personality of Salis's cabaret, and of the young artists who filled it. Allais also decided to present himself strictly as a humorist, jettisoning his romantic and gothic tales, and picking a title suitable for a joke book.

It was an astute move, for the next year he was invited to write a regular column for *Le Journal*. His new paper had a wider circulation, which meant more money, but also meant that he had to adjust his style. Francisque Sarcey still waddled and pontificated through the columns, but not over his own signature. The pieces became shorter and more topical.

Allais continued to write for *Le Journal* until his death, collecting his columns every year or so into the books he called his "anthumous works." In 1899 he also became editor of another paper, *Le Sourire*, and continued to turn out several pieces a week for both papers until his death in 1906. He was only 52, worn down by deadlines, a bad marriage, financial troubles, and alcohol.

Some of the stories here have been translated before, but not the whole book as Allais planned it. I've provided footnotes, placed discreetly in the back, for some of the topical or cultural references. Many of the characters in his pieces were real people of the time, who have been briefly identified in the notes. I made no attempt to translate any of the fictional characters' names; I glossed any joke names in the notes. Four pieces ("As Good a Way as Any," "The Doctor," "The Calf," and "An Invention") appeared previously in my edition of Allais's *Selected Plays*, published in 2014 by Black Scat Books. To mollify repeat customers, I've added seven stories also taken from *Le Chat Noir*. Some are fine specimens of the romantic and supernatural tales Allais sometimes wrote before plumping strictly for laughs; others show him trying out different comic gambits. They're all Allais, having the time of his life in Montmartre.

Doug Skinner
New Paltz, NY
September, 2016

A Philosopher

I grew quite fond of that big lazy customs official, who seemed the perfect image of customs, not the churlish customs of our terrestrial borders, but the good old idle and contemplative customs of our cliffs and seashore.

His name was Pascal; it should have been Baptiste, so much gentle tranquility did he bring to everything he did in life. And it was a pleasure to see him, his hands clasped behind his back, slowly dawdling through his three hours of duty on the wharfs, preferably those with only disused boats and unarmed yachts.

As soon as his work was over, Pascal quickly shed his blue trousers and green tunic to don cotton overalls and a long shirt, which countless sunstrokes and diluvian floods (perhaps even antediluvian) had given that special shade found only on the backs of fishermen. For Pascal was an angler, like the ancient Anglo-Saxons. Nobody was better at finding the good spots in ponds, and at baiting judiciously, with an earthworm, a cooked shrimp, a raw shrimp, or any other treacherous foodstuff.

Obliging, besides, and always willing to give advice to beginners. And so it was that we quickly got to know one another.

One thing about him intrigued me; it was that sort of

little class that he brought along every day: three boys and two girls, all different in age and appearance.

His children? No, for not the slightest family resemblance could be discerned in their faces. Probably neighborhood children, then.

Pascal arranged the five kids with the greatest care, the youngest next to him, the oldest at the other end.

And all of this little crowd began fishing like grown men, with a serious air that was so comical that I couldn't look at them without laughing.

What I also found amusing was the way in which Pascal designated each of the kids.

Instead of giving them their baptismal names, as is usually done, Eugene, Victor, or Emily, he attributed to each a profession or nationality.

There was the *Sub-Inspector*, the *Norwegian*, the *Broker*, the *Insurance Agent*, and the *Reverend Father*.

The *Sub-Inspector* was the oldest, and the *Reverend Father* the littlest.

The children, besides, seemed used to these titles, and when Pascal said, "*Sub-Inspector*, go get me four sous of tobacco," the *Sub-Inspector* gravely arose and accomplished his mission without the slightest surprise.

One day, as I was walking along the beach, I met my friend Pascal on duty, his arms crossed, his rifle slung over his shoulder, sadly contemplating the sun, which was ready to set, over there, in the sea.

"A lovely spectacle, Pascal!"

"Superb! Once never tires of it."

"Are you a poet?"

"Good Lord, no! I'm just a simple customs official, but that doesn't stop me from admiring nature."

Good old Pascal! We had a long talk, and I finally learned the origin of the bizarre appellations he attached to his young fishing companions.

"When I married my wife, she worked as a maid for the Sub-Inspector. It was even he who convinced me to marry her. He knew quite well what he was doing, the scoundrel, because six months later she gave birth to our oldest, the one I call the *Sub-Inspector*, as is only right. A year later, my wife had a little daughter who looked so much like a tall young Norwegian who had hired her to clean for him, that I had not a minute of doubt. That one is the *Norwegian*. And then, every year, it continued. Not that my wife is more immoral than any other, but she's too kind-hearted. People like that don't know how to say no. In short, I have seven children, and only the last one is mine."

"And you call that one the *Customs Official*, I suppose?"

"No, I call him the *Cuckold*, that's nicer."

Winter came; I had to leave Houlbec, but not without bidding an affectionate farewell to my friend Pascal and to all his little functionaries. I even offered them small gifts, which filled them with joy.

The next year, I returned to Houlbec to spend the summer.

The very day of my arrival, I met the *Norwegian*, on her way to do some errands.

How pretty she had become, that little *Norwegian*!

With her big sea-green eyes and her light golden hair, she looked like one of those blonde fairies from Scandinavian legend. She recognized me and ran up to me.

I kissed her:

"Hello, *Norwegian*, how are you?"

"Very well, sir, thank you."

"And your papa?"

"Very well, sir, thank you."

"And your mama, your little sister, your little brothers?"

"Everyone's fine, sir, thank you. The *Cuckold* had the measles this winter, but he's completely cured now... and then, last week, mama gave birth to a little *Justice of the Peace*."

Ferdinand

Do animals have souls? Why wouldn't they? I've met, in my life, a considerable quantity of men, including several women, who were as dumb as geese, and numerous animals no stupider than many voters.

And even—I don't claim that it happens often—I have personally known a duck with a touch of genius.

This duck, called Ferdinand, in honor of the great Frenchman, was born in the barnyard belonging to my godfather, the Marquis of Belveau, president of the organizing committee for the "General Society for Billposting in Tunnels."

It was on my godfather's property that I spent all my vacations, since my parents practiced an unhealthy business in a confined space.

(My parents—I prefer to say this now, so they can't be accused of indifference toward me—had established a phosphorus refinery in a sixth floor apartment, rue des Blancs-Manteaux, consisting of a room, a kitchen, and a storage space that served as a salon.)

A veritable Eden, my godfather's property! But it was the barnyard I liked the best, probably because it was the dirtiest place in the area.

There one could find, living in poignant fraternity, an adult pig, rabbits of all ages, polychromatic fowls, and ducks worthy to kneel before, so much did their song equal their plumage.

And there I met Ferdinand, who was, at the time, a young duck about two or three months old. Ferdinand and I soon grew quite fond of one another.

As soon as I arrived, there were quacks of welcome, shaking of wings, a whole noisy testimony of friendship that went straight to my heart.

The thought of Ferdinand's upcoming finish froze my heart with despair.

Ferdinand was well aware of his fate, *conscius sui fati*. When he was given turnip peelings or pea pods in his food, a bitter rictus twisted the corners of his beak, and a sort of cloud of death veiled, in advance, his little yellow eyes.

Fortunately, Ferdinand was not a duck to let himself be spitted like some common turkey. "Since I'm not the strongest," he told himself, "I'll be the cleverest," and he worked to avoid ever experiencing the high temperatures of the saucepan or the grill.

He had noticed the cook's usual practice, whenever she needed a subject from the barnyard. The cruel woman seized the animal, weighed it, and carefully squeezed it: the ultimate groping!

Ferdinand swore never to grow fat, and kept his word.

He ate very little, never any starches, and avoided drinking at meals, as advised by the best doctors. Plenty of exercise.

When this treatment was not sufficient, Ferdinand, aided by his instincts and a rare aptitude for natural science, invaded the garden at night and ingested the most purgative plants, the most drastic roots.

For some time, his efforts were crowned with success, but his poor duck's body grew used to the drugs, and my unfortunate Ferdinand soon regained his lost weight.

He tried poisonous plants in small doses, and sucked a few leaves of a *Datura stramonium*, which played a decorative and thorny role in my godfather's shrubbery.

Ferdinand was as sick as a strong horse, and barely survived.

Electricity suggested itself to his ingenious soul, and I often surprised him with his eyes lifted to the telegraph wires that striped the azure, just above the barnyard; but his poor atrophied wings refused to fly to such a height.

One day, the cook, impatient with this stubborn emaciation, seized Ferdinand and tied his feet, murmuring, "Bah, in the saucepan, with a good dollop of fresh peas!..."

Space is lacking to describe my consternation.

Ferdinand would see the light of only one more dawn.

At night, I arose to bid my friend a final adieu, and this is the spectacle that met my eyes:

Ferdinand, his feet still tied, had dragged himself to the threshold of the kitchen. With energetic alternating strokes, he sharpened his beak on the granite step. Then, with one sharp blow, he cut the restraining string, and found himself once again on his legs, now somewhat stiff.

Thoroughly reassured, I returned quietly to my room, and fell fast asleep.

The next morning, you cannot imagine the cries that filled the house. The cook, in malicious, vulgar, and tempestuous language, announced Ferdinand's escape to us all.

"Madame! Madame! Ferdinand's buggered off!"

Five minutes later, a new discovery put her beside herself:

"Madame! Madame! Just imagine! That little pig gobbled up all the peas I was going to serve with him!"

With that detail, I easily recognized my good old Ferdinand.

What happened to him, after that?

Perhaps he put to evil use the marvelous faculties that nature, *alma parens*, delighted to bestow upon him.

What does it matter? I shall always remember Ferdinand as a wily little rascal.

And so will you, I hope!

Customs of the Times

Both very industrious and very bohemian, he divides his time between the studio and the bar, between his vast studio on the Boulevard Clichy and the gay cabarets of Montmartre.

His social polish therefore has remained thoroughly embryonic.

Recently, he had a portrait to paint, the portrait of a lady, a very important lady, a high baroness of finance who was also an exquisite Parisienne.

And he acquitted himself admirably.

She appeared on canvas as she is in life, that is to say, charming and delectable, with an indefinable hint of passion.

At the next Salon, after having consulted a disappointing catalogue, everyone will murmur, a bit troubled:

"I'd like to know who that baroness is."

And she was so satisfied with her portrait that she gave the painter a dinner in his honor, a big dinner.

At the beginning of the meal, he was somewhat uncomfortable in his unfamiliar frock coat, but he eventually grew used to it.

At dessert, if he only had his pipe, his good old pipe, he

would have been completely happy.

The espresso was served in the machine, a marvelous machine in which the industry of the Orient apparently had a rendezvous with the spirit of the Tropics.

He is totally at ease now, and gives free rein to his merriest paradoxes, which the guests listen to seriously, with a touch of bewilderment.

Then, while chatting, as the baroness refills his glass with an infinitely old cognac, he seizes his neighbors' saucers and piles them before him.

And as the baroness contemplates this performance, not without surprise, he says, quite politely:

"I insist, Baroness: this round's on me."

On the Town

The young and brilliant artillery sergeant Raoul de Montcocasse is radiant. He has just been entrusted with a mission which, while flattering his officer's ego, assures him that the next day will be one of those happy ones important in a gunner's existence.

He is to go to Saint-Cloud with three men, to take possession of a piece of artillery and to bring it back to the fort at Vincennes.

Be assured, compassionate readers, that this story takes place in peacetime, and, throughout these pages, our friend Raoul will be in no serious danger.

At dawn, everyone was ready, and the little cavalcade set off. Superb weather!

"A fine day!" said Raoul, as he stroked his horse's neck.

When he said "fine day," Raoul had no idea how right he was, because for a fine day, it was a fine day.

They arrived at Saint-Cloud without trouble, but with such an appetite! The appetite of a gunner who dreams that his shells are made of mortadella!

Feeling flush that day, Raoul offered his men a copious lunch at the Green Noggin. As they smoked fine cigars, they had a fine cup of coffee and a fine pousse-café, itself followed with several more pousse-cafés, and they were all quite flushed when they thought about attending to the delivery of the piece in question.

"Let's not make ourselves late," remarked Raoul.

I believe that I observed above that it was a fine day; now, one can't have a fine day without a little heat, and heat is well known for provoking thirst in the army in general, and particularly in the artillery, which is an elite group.

Fortunately Providence, which oversees everything, sprinkled the banks of the Seine with an appreciable number of joyful saloons, moisteners that never tired of parched throats.

Raoul and his men absorbed oceans of that little Argenteuil that evokes more the idea of a sapphire than a ruby, and which enters your stomach like a corkscrew.

They arrived at the fortifications.

"No nonsense, now!" ordered the dignified Montcocasse. "Here we are in town."

And the gunners, suddenly suffused with a sense of duty, applied themselves to assuming decorative attitudes, in keeping with the mission they were to accomplish.

The cannon itself, a fine De Bange 90 mm, seemed to double in seriousness.

As they crossed the Pont Royal, Raoul remembered that nearby, in the faubourg Saint-Germain, lived an aunt of his, whom he had saddened by his youthful excesses.

"Now's the time," he said to himself, "to show her that I've made something of myself."

At full gallop, with a terrifying clatter of bronze on the stones of the rue de l'Université, they arrived at the old hotel of Montcocasses's dowager.

Everyone was at the window, the dowager with the rest.

Raoul made his horse prance, unsheathed his saber, and, seizing his kepi as if it were some plumed cocked hat, saluted his startled aunt—like those valiant knights who had no ancestors—and disappeared, he, his men, and his cannon, like in a dream.

The little troop, still at full gallop, turned onto rue Vaugirard, and soon found themselves at the Odéon.

At that point, there was a bottleneck. An omnibus, Panthéon-Place Courcelles, lay scattered on the ground, an axle broken.

All of the little ladies of the Brasserie Médicis were at the door, delighted by the accident.

Raoul, who had been one of their best customers, was recognized immediately:

"Raoul! Hey Raoul! Come down from your horse, hey you lazybones!"

Although not actually a "lazybones," Raoul came down from his horse, and thought that he could not pass by the Médicis without buying the ladies a round.

With the charming solidarity of the Latin Quarter

women, Nana strongly advised Raoul to go see Camille, at the Ferret. She'd enjoy that.

In fact, Camille did enjoy seeing her friend Raoul in such a fine getup.

"You must go say hello to Palmyre, at the Cuckoo. She'd enjoy that."

They went to say hello to Palmyre, who sent Raoul to say hello to Renée, at the Pantagruel.

Docile and noisy, the good old cannon followed the party, looking a bit astonished at the unusual role it was forced to play.

The little ladies had the mechanism of the murderous engine explained to them, and Blanche, of the Harcourt, even made a remark that bellicose monarchs might well consider:

"Men must be stupid to make machines like that, to kill each other... as if we didn't kick the bucket soon enough already!"

From bock to cognac, from cognac to absinthe, from absinthe to bitters, they gradually arrived at seven in the evening.

It was too late to return. They dined in the Latin Quarter and spent the evening there.

The police started to become concerned about the noisy cannon, and about those steaming horses they met on every disreputable street.

But what do you expect the police to do against the artillery?

At break of day, Raoul, his men, and his cannon made a modest entrance into the fort at Vincennes.

At the risk of disturbing the sensitive reader, I will add that poor Raoul was demoted and sentenced to a few weeks in prison.

Following this adventure, completely disgusted with the artillery, he was permitted to join a regiment of Spahis, where he soon became its most brilliant ornament.

As Good A Way As Any

—Once upon a time there was an uncle and a nephew.

—Which one was the uncle?

—What do you mean, which one? The fatter one, of course!

—So uncles are fat?

—Often.

—But my Uncle Henri isn't fat.

—Your Uncle Henri isn't fat because he's an artist.

—So artists aren't fat?

—You're bothering me... If you keep interrupting, I can't tell my story.

—I won't interrupt, go ahead.

—Once upon a time there was an uncle and a nephew. The uncle was very rich, very rich.

—How much money did he have?

—Seventeen hundred billion in income, plus houses, carriages, lands...

— And horses?

—Why, of course, since he had carriages.

—And boats? Did he have boats?

—Yes, forty of them.

—Steamboats?

—Three were steamboats, and the rest had sails.

—And his nephew, did he go on the boat?

—Stop it! You won't let me tell the story.

—Go ahead, tell it, I won't bother you any more.

—The nephew, however, didn't have a sou, and that irritated him enormously.

—Why didn't his uncle give him some?

—Because his uncle was an old miser who liked to keep his money for himself. But since the nephew was his only heir...

—What's an "heir"?

—Those are the people who take your money, your furniture, everything that you own, when you're dead.

—So why didn't the nephew kill the uncle?

—Well, you're a nice one, aren't you? He didn't kill his uncle because you should never kill your uncle, under any circumstances, even for an inheritance.

—Why should you never kill your uncle?

—Because of the police.

—But what if they don't find out?

—The police always find out, the concierge tells them. And besides, you'll see that the nephew was more clever than that. He had noticed that after every meal, his uncle became quite red...

—Maybe he was drunk.

—No, it was his physical condition. He was apoplectic.

—What's "aplopecpit"?

—Apoplectic... Those are people whose blood goes to their heads, and who could die from a strong emotion.

—Am I apoplectic?

—No, and you never will be. You're not the type. So, the nephew had noticed that laughter made his uncle particularly ill, and that once he had almost died after a prolonged fit of laughter.

—Does laughter make you die?

—Yes, if you're apoplectic. One fine day, the nephew arrives at his uncle's house just as his uncle is leaving the table. Never had he eaten so well. He was as red as a rooster, and was puffing like a seal...

—Like the seals in the zoo at the Bois de Boulogne?

—No, those aren't seals, they're sea lions. The nephew says to himself, "Now's the time," and he starts to tell a funny, funny story.

—Will you tell it to me?

—Wait a moment, I'll tell it at the end... The uncle listened to the story, and he laughed, he doubled over laughing, so much that he died of laughter even before the story was finished.

—So, what was the story he told him?

—Wait a minute... Then, when the uncle was dead, they buried him, and the nephew inherited everything.

—Did he get the boats, too?

—He got everything, because he was the only heir.

—But what was the story he told his uncle?

—Why, the one I just told you.

—Which one?

—The one about the uncle and the nephew.

—You old joker!

—And what about you, eh?

Collage

Dr. Joris-Abraham-W. Snowdrop, of Pigtown (U.S.A.), had reached the age of fifty-five, and none of his friends or family had convinced him to take a wife.

Last year, a few days before Christmas, he entered the department store on 37th Square (*Artistic Objects in Banaloid*), to buy his Christmas presents.

The person who served the doctor was a tall young redhead, so infinitely charming that he felt the first stirrings of his life. At the cashier, he learned the name of the young lady.

"Miss Bertha."

He asked Miss Bertha if she would like to marry him. Miss Bertha replied that naturally ("of course") she would.

Two weeks after they met, the seductive Miss Bertha became the beautiful Mrs. Snowdrop.

Despite his fifty-five years, the doctor was a perfectly presentable husband. Beautiful silver hair framed his handsome face, which was always scrupulously shaven.

He was mad about his young wife, very attentive, and touchingly gentle with her.

And yet, the evening of their marriage, he had told her with terrible calm:

"Bertha, if you are ever unfaithful to me, make sure that I never know."

And he had added:

"In your own interest."

Dr. Snowdrop, like many American doctors, had living with him a student who attended his consultations and accompanied his house calls, an excellent practical education that should be instituted in France. We might see a decline in the mortality that so cruelly afflicts our young doctors' clientele.

Dr. Snowdrop's student, George Arthurson, a handsome lad of about twenty, was the son of one of the doctor's oldest friends, and the doctor loved him like his own son.

The young man was not insensible to Miss Bertha's beauty, but being a decent young man, he suppressed his feelings to the bottom of his heart, and threw himself into his studies to occupy his mind.

Bertha, on her part, had loved George at once, but, being a faithful wife, wanted to wait for George to make the first move.

The situation could not long endure, and one fine day George and Bertha found themselves in each other's arms.

Ashamed of his weakness, George swore not to continue, but Bertha had sworn the opposite.

The young man avoided her; she wrote him letters overflowing with passion:

"...*To be with you always; never to leave you; to make our two beings into one!...*"

The letter in which this passage blazed fell into the hands of the doctor, who contented himself with murmuring:

"That can be arranged."

That very evening, they dined at White Oak Park, a property the doctor owned near Pigtown.

During the meal, a strange and uncontrollable torpor came over the two lovers.

With the assistance of Joe, an athletic Negro who had worked for him since the Civil War, Snowdrop undressed the guilty couple, laid them on the same bed, and completed their anesthesia with a certain hydrocarbon of his own invention.

He prepared his surgical instruments as calmly as if he were only cutting a corn from a Chinese.

Then, with truly remarkable dexterity, he removed, by dislocating them, his wife's right arm and right leg.

From George, by the same operation, he removed the left arm and left leg.

All along Bertha's right side, all along George's left side, he removed a strip of skin about three inches wide.

Then, joining the two bodies so that the open wounds joined, he kept them glued to each other, very firmly, with a long strip of canvas that he wrapped a hundred times around the young couple.

During the entire operation, Bertha and George never moved.

After verifying that they were in stable condition, the doctor introduced into their stomachs, thanks to an esophageal probe, nutritious broth and old Bordeaux.

Under the influence of skillfully administered narcotics, they remained like that for fifteen days.

On the sixteenth day, the doctor noted that all was going well.

The incisions on their shoulders and thighs had healed.

As for their two sides, they now formed only one.

Then Snowdrop had a gleam of triumph in his eyes, and he discontinued the narcotics.

Awakened at the same time, George and Bertha believed themselves the victims of some hideous nightmare.

But it was even more terrible when they saw that it was not a dream.

The doctor couldn't help smiling at the sight.

As for Joe, he was splitting his sides.

Bertha, especially, howled like a mad hyena.

"What are you complaining about, my dear?" Snowdrop gently interrupted. "I did nothing but grant your fondest wish: '...*To be with you always; never to leave you; to make our two beings into one!...*'"

And with a slight smile, the doctor added:

"It's what the French call *collage*."

Little Pigs

Bitter disappointment awaited me in Andouilly.

The little town that was so joyous, so elegant, so bright, where I had once spent the happiest six months of my existence, gave me immediately, as soon as I arrived, the effect of the "sad village" described by the poet Capus.

A great shroud of affliction seemed to envelop everybody and everything.

Yet the weather was fine, and nothing in my mood that day predisposed me to see the world as so dreary.

"Bah!" I said to myself. "It's just a little cloud floating in the sky of my brain, and it will pass."

I entered the Market Cafe, which was, at one time, my cafe of predilection. Not one of the old regulars was there, even though it was almost noon.

The waiter was not the old waiter. As for the boss, he was a new boss, and the boss's wife was different too, as is only right.

I inquired:

"M. Fourquemin is no longer here?"

"Oh, no sir, since three months ago. M. Fourquemin is in the Good Savior asylum, and Mme Fourquemin has started a little dry goods store in Dozulé, where her parents are from."

"Has M. Fourquemin gone mad?"

"Not raving mad, but so obsessive they had to lock him up."

"What obsession does he have?"

"Oh, a very odd obsession, sir. Just imagine: he can't see a piece of bread without wanting to tear off a chunk to make into little pigs."

"What are you telling me?"

"The plain truth, sir, and what's even more curious is that this strange illness has raged throughout the area like an epidemic. In the Good Savior asylum alone, there are some thirty people from Andouilly who spend their days making little pigs from bread, and little pigs that are so small, sir, that you need a magnifying glass to look at them. There's a name for this disease. It's called... It's called... What the devil did that Parisian doctor say, M. Romain?"

M. Romain, sipping his aperitif at a nearby table, responded with courtesy mixed with pretension:

"*Delphacomania*, sir, from the Greek word *delphax, delphacos*, which means little pig."

"Besides," continued the proprietor, "if you want the details, you can simply inquire at the France and Normandy Hotel. That's where the trouble began."

The France and Normandy Hotel, in fact, was my hotel, and I decided to lunch there.

When I entered the restaurant, everyone was seated, and, among the guests, not one familiar face.

The employee of the highways department, the postal worker, the member of the Board of Internal Economy, the representative of the *National*, all those fine lads whom I had so often toasted, all gone, dispersed, perhaps all in padded cells as well?

My heart was gripped as if in a vice.

The proprietor recognized me, and held out his hand, sadly, without a word.

"Well, what happened?" I said.

"Ah, M. Ludovic, what a tragedy for everyone, beginning with me!"

And since I insisted, he told me quietly:

"I'll tell you after lunch, because the story might influence our new guests."

After lunch, this is what I learned:

The restaurant in the France and Normandy Hotel is frequented by bachelors who belong, for the most part, to government administrations and insurance companies, by traveling salesmen, etc., etc. In general, they're well educated young men, who often become rather bored in Andouilly, a pretty region, but a bit monotonous in the long run.

The arrival of a new guest, traveling salesman, tourist,

or anyone else is therefore seen as a stroke of luck: he's a breath of fresh air come to gently ruffle the dreary and stagnant pond of daily tedium.

They chat, they linger over dessert, they show each other tricks, they balance forks, plates, bottles. They tell the joke about the man from Marseille:

"Do you know this one? It seems there was a man from Marseille..."

In short, these few distractions make the time pass more quickly, and even the least agreeable stranger finds a friendly welcome.

Well, one day, there arrived a young man of about thirty, whose business consisted of renting empty shops in different towns, and selling jewelry at fabulously cheap prices.

To give you an idea of his prices, he offered a silver watch for almost nothing. Clocks were not much more expensive.

This young man, of Swiss nationality, was named Henri Jouard. Like all Swiss, Jouard added the patience of a marmot to the dexterity of a marmoset.

The young man was as composed as a rabbit, and as sweet and gentle as a shoulder of mutton.

What then, dear Lord, could have led anyone to suspect, at that time, that this Helvetian could have unleashed on Andouilly the pitiless torrent of delphacomania?

Every evening after dinner, Jouard, as he drank his coffee, had the habit of modeling little pigs from bread.

The little pigs, it must be admitted, were marvelous little pigs: little turned-up tail, little feet, and a pretty little snout, all cleverly executed.

He made the eyes with the tip of a burned match, applied to the proper place. That gave it pretty little black ones.

Naturally, everyone started making pigs. They warmed to the task, and a few of the hotel guests became quite adept in the art. One of these gentlemen, a certain Vallée, a tax administrator, was particularly successful in this exercise.

One evening when they had almost run out of bread, Vallée made a little pig whose total length, from its snout to the tip of its tail, was under one centimeter.

Everyone openly admired it. Only Jouard respectfully shrugged his shoulders, saying:

"With the same amount of bread, I can make two pigs."

And, kneading Vallée's pig, he made two from it.

Vallée, somewhat annoyed, took the two pigs and quickly confected three.

Meanwhile, the other guests applied themselves, imperturbably serious, to modeling minuscule pigs.

It was getting late; they all left.

The next day, at lunch, each guest, without a word, drew from his pocket a little box containing tiny pigs infinitely more minuscule than those from the day before.

They had all spent their mornings on this exercise, in their respective offices.

Jouard promised to bring, that very evening, a pig that would be the last word in microscopic pigs.

He brought it, but Vallée also brought one, and Vallée's pig was even smaller than Jouard's, and better realized.

This success encouraged the younger men, whose sole occupation after that was kneading little pigs, at every hour of the day, at the table, in the cafe, and especially in the office. Public services suffered cruelly from it, and taxpayers complained to the government, or wrote letters to the *Lantern* and the *Little Parisian*.

Changes, scandals, and dismissals embellished the *Official*.

All in vain! Delphacomania does not so easily release its prey.

The worst part of the situation was that the disease spread to the town. Young salesmen, shopkeepers, M. Fourquemin himself, the proprietor of the Market Cafe, fell victim to the epidemic. All of Andouilly molded little pigs whose weight averaged less than a milligram.

Business declined, industry faltered, administration stagnated!

Without the initiative of the prefect, Andouilly would have been finished.

But the prefect, who found himself to be M. Rivaud, currently the prefect of Rhône, took measures that bordered on savagery.

Andouilly was saved, but how long will it take this little town, once so flourishing, to regain its prosperity and cheerful tranquility?

Cruel Enigma

Every evening, after I've missed the last train for Maisons-Lafitte (and Lord knows if this adventure happens to me more than is my share), I spend the night in a *pied-à-terre* that I keep in Paris.

It's a humble dwelling, peaceful and honest, like the dwelling of the boy into whose head Napoleon III, then a simple president of the Republic, lodged three bullets so that he could ascend the throne.

There is, however, no holy laurel above a portrait, and no old weeping grandmother.

Fortunately!

My *pied-à-terre*, I prefer to tell you right away, is a simple room bearing the number 80, situated in the Three Hemispheres Hotel, rue des Victimes.

Extremely clean and perfectly maintained, the establishment is ideal for single gentlemen, families traveling through Paris, or those who, living in the city, are denuded of furniture.

Under his grumbling and sullen exterior, the proprietor, M. Stéphany, hides a heart of gold. His wife is the friendliest and cheeriest hotelkeeper in the kingdom.

And besides, in the office there is often a woman named

Marie, who is very nice. (She's been a bit ill these past few days, but is much better now, thank you.)

The Three Hemispheres Hotel has this to say for it: it is international, cosmopolitan, and even polyglot.

Ever since I began staying there, I've started to believe in geography, because until now—must I admit it?—geography has always seemed to me like a good "gag."

In this hostelry, the most chimerical nations seem determined to meet each other.

And there is, in the corridors, a confusion of jargons, of which the tower built by the engineer Babel, admittedly picturesque, could give but a feeble notion.

Last month, a clown from the Faroe Islands met, in the stairway, a young Armenian of great beauty.

She showed such grace in carrying her four sous of milk in her tin cup, that the islander fell madly in love with her.

To obtain her parents' consent, they telegraphed the young woman's father, then traveling in Thuringia, and her mother, who was staying not far from the kingdom of Siam.

Fortunately, the fiance had never met his parents, because one wonders where they might have had to look for those two.

The marriage was celebrated recently in the town hall of the XVIIIth. M. Bin, at the time both mayor and priest of his arrondissement, took advantage of the situation to "reel off" a little speech on the unity of nations, declaring that he was resolutely determined to maintain peaceful relations with Batignolles, as well as with la Chapelle and Ménilmontant.

......

I mentioned above that my door bears the number 80. It is therefore next to 81.

For several days, 81 had been vacant.

One evening, on returning, I discovered that I had a new neighbor, or rather neighboress.

Was my neighboress pretty? I had no idea, but what I could affirm was that she sang adorably. (The walls of my hotel are constructed, I believe, from simple onionskin.)

She must have been young, for the timbre of her voice was deliciously fresh, with something, in the lower notes, that was strange and profoundly moving.

She sang a simple traditional American tune, of which there are so many exquisite examples.

Soon the song came to a close, and a man's voice was heard:

"Bravo, Miss Ellen! You sing beautifully, and have given me the keenest pleasure... And you, master Sem, won't you give us a song from your country too?"

A rough gravelly voice replied, in Negro-American dialect:

"If you would enjoy that, M. George."

And the old Negro (for he was obviously an old Negro) struck up a comical ditty, accompanying the chorus by dancing a jig, to the great joy of the young woman, who responded with shrill peals of laughter.

"It's your turn, Doddy," the man said. "Tell us one of those lovely stories that you tell so well."

And little Doddy recited a lovely story at such a precipitous speed that I could only make out a few vague phrases.

"That was very pretty," the man replied. "Since you've all been so good, I'll play you a little tune on the guitar, after which we'll all take a nice nap."

The man charmed me with his guitar.

For my taste, he stopped too soon, for the room fell into absolute silence.

"How," I asked myself, baffled, "can all four of them spend the night in such a small room?"

And I tried to figure out their arrangement.

Miss Ellen slept with George.

They improvised a bed for little Doddy, and Sem stretched out on the floor. (Those old Negroes have seen worse!)

Ellen! What a pretty voice, all the same!

And I fell asleep, my head filled with Ellen.

The next day, I woke to a terrible racket. It was master

Sem, who stretched out his legs by executing one of his national jigs.

This entertainment was followed by a little song from Doddy, an adorable ballad from Miss Ellen, and a truly masterful cornet solo.

Suddenly, a voice arose from the courtyard:

"Hey George! Are you ready? I'm waiting!"

"All right, all right, let me brush my hat and I'll be right down."

Sure enough, a minute later, George left.

I opened my door a crack to take a look at him.

He was a tall young man, clean shaven, properly dressed, a thorough gentleman.

In the room, all was quiet.

I listened in vain; I heard nothing.

They must have gone back to sleep, I thought.

And yet, that devilish Sem had seemed wide awake.

What peculiar people!

It was about nine o'clock. I waited.

Minutes passed, then quarter hours, then hours. Still no movement.

It would soon be noon.

The silence became disturbing.

I had an idea.

I shot off a revolver in my room, and listened.

Not a cry, not a murmur, not a remark from my neighbors.

I then became seriously afraid.

I went to knock on their door:

"Open the door, Sem!... Miss Ellen!... Doddy! Open the door!..."

Nothing stirred!

There could be no more doubt, they were all dead.

Murdered by George, perhaps!

Or asphyxiated!

I wanted to look through the keyhole.

The key was in the door.

I didn't dare enter.

Like a madman, I rushed to the front desk.

"Madame Stéphany," I asked, trying to sound indifferent, "who's in the room next to me?"

"In 81? An American, M. George Huyotson."

"And what does he do?"

"He's a ventriloquist."

The Doctor

Monologue for Cadet

For sheer nerve, there's nobody like a doctor. Infernal nerve! And contempt for human life, as well!

You're sick, your doctor comes. He palpates you, he auscultates you, he interrogates you, all while thinking of something else. Once his prescription is written, he says, "I'll return," and—you can be sure of it—that he will, once you've passed the point of *no* return.

When you die, an undertaker comes at once to bring him a little kickback for the funeral.

If you prove resistant to the illness, and especially to his prescriptions, the doctor rubs his hands, because his little visits, and his cut from the pharmacist in particular, start to snowball, and become quite a tidy sum.

Only one thing bothers the good doctor: that's when you get well quickly. Even then, he finds a way to work his mischief, and says, with infernal aplomb:

"Aha! I pulled you out of that one!"

But the doctor who has the most nerve of all is mine; or rather ex-mine, because I got rid of him, and, believe me, I didn't regret it.

After I had been too cold and then too hot—or too hot

and then too cold, I don't remember—I became somewhat indisposed. Hoping to save my skin—what do you expect, it's the only one I have—I called my doctor, who arrived promptly.

I was already feeling bad, but after his first prescription, I took a definite turn for the worse, and had to stay in bed.

Another visit, another prescription, another downturn.

In short, after four days, I'd lost several pounds... even kilos.

One morning when I was feeling not at all well, my doctor, after auscultating me more carefully than usual, asked me:

"Are you content with this apartment?"

"Why, yes, pretty much."

"How much is your rent?"

"Three thousand and four."

"Is the concierge acceptable?"

"I've never had any complaints."

"And the landlord?"

"The landlord is very nice."

"Do the chimneys smoke?"

"Not much."

Etc., etc.

And I wondered, "What is this character driving at?" Whether my apartment is humid or not, that might have some bearing on my illness, but how much rent I pay? What does that have to do with him? And despite my weakened condition, I ventured to ask:

"But doctor, why all of these questions?"

"I'll tell you," he replied. "I'm looking for an apartment, and yours would suit me perfectly."

"But... I have no plans to move!"

"And yet you'll have to in a few days."

"To move?"

"Something like that."

And I understood!

My doctor considered my condition serious, and made that rather clear.

I can't express the effect of this sudden revelation, not in any language.

Terrible anxiety at first, stark terror!

And then, white-hot rage! You don't act like that with a sick man, with a client, and a good client, I must say.

Ah! You want my apartment, my friend? Well, nothing doing!

.....

The next time you're sick, let me recommend this procedure: get angry. For you, it might make you worse. For me, it cured me.

I kicked my doctor out the door.

I threw my medications out the window.

When I say that I threw them out the window, I

exaggerate. I don't like to break glass on purpose; it could hurt people walking by, and I don't want to hurt people: I'm no doctor!

I contented myself with sending all my bottles back to the pharmacist, with a stern note.

There were so many bottles, so many packets and boxes!

There were so many, that one day I made a mistake: I put syrup on my stomach, and swallowed a plaster.

In fact, it was the only time I got any relief.

After that, I renewed my lease, and never consulted a doctor again.

Boisflambard

The last time I ran into Boisflambard, it was early one morning (I can't remember why on earth I got up so early), at the corner of boulevard Saint-Michel and rue Racine.

My poor Boisflambard, *quantum mutatus*!

At that time, young Boisflamard epitomized all the elegance of the Latin Quarter.

A handsome fellow, nicely put together, Maurice Boisflambard strove to be the best dressed man on the whole left bank.

The polish of his boots had no serious competition but the shine on his hats, and if we never tired of admiring his ties, we had long ago given up counting them.

The same for his waistcoats.

What did Boisflambard do in the Latin Quarter? That was something nobody could say, exactly. Student? Student of what, and at what moment of the day could he have studied? What courses, what clinics, could he have followed?

For during the day, Boisflambard only frequented brasseries; in the evening, only the Bullier dancehall, or an enormously noisy concert hall, now gone, called the Chalet.

But what did we care about Boisflambard's social function? Wasn't he the best fellow in the world, charming, obliging, friendly to all?

Poor Boisflambard!

It took me a few long seconds to recognize him, so much did his pitiful appearance contrast with his usual dandyism.

Thick shoes, well polished, but showing, in several places, serious claims for retirement; poor old frayed black gloves; a common cotton shirt that was irreproachably clean, but clumsily made, and patched in a thousand places; a more than modest tie that seemed to come from some distant village; the whole completed by a red top hat and a green frock coat.

In the interest of truth, I should add that the red top hat and green frock coat had both been black in days gone by.

And incidentally, who can tell me why Time, that great colorist, amuses itself by turning hats red, and frock coats green? Nature is capricious: she abhors a vacuum, perhaps she has a keen penchant for complementary colors!

I shook Boisflambard's hand; but, despite my best efforts, my face reflected an astonishment that did not escape my friend.

He became as red as a rooster (a red rooster, of course).

"My friend," he stammered, "you must understand,

from my appearance, that an irreparable misfortune has befallen me. You won't see me again: I leave Paris at once."

I found no reply but a handshake, into which I put all of my cordiality.

Turning more and more scarlet, Boisflambard disappeared in the direction of rue Racine.

Since that meeting, I've often wondered what happened to the unfortunate Boisflambard, and my ideas, on that subject, took two different turns.

First, a sincere and friendly compassion for his misfortune, and then a legitimate astonishment at the sudden physical effect the catastrophe had on inanimate objects, like his shoes or shirt.

That a man could be so stricken by calamity, that his hair turn white overnight, I admit willingly; but that the same calamity could transform, in one week, a pair of elegant boots into a coachman's shoes, that surpassed my understanding.

And yet, at last, a thought came to me, which brought some peace to my troubled mind: perhaps Boisflambard had sold his sumptuous wardrobe to replace it with more modest attire?

A few years after this adventure, I suffered an injury in a small town in the country.

Clinging to the upper deck of a coach, I didn't wait for

the ladder to be positioned. I jumped to the ground and twisted my ankle.

I was carried into a hotel room, and, as I awaited the doctor, my foot was wrapped in a prodigious quantity of compresses, enough to make me think that all of the hotel's linen went into my bandage.

"Ah, here's the doctor!" cried one of the maids.

I lifted my head, and could not suppress a cry of delighted surprise.

The man they called the "doctor" was my old comrade Boisflambard.

A Boisflambard who was a bit heavier, but elegant all the same, and as superbly dressed as in his glory days in the Latin Quarter.

"Boisflambard!"

"You!"

"What are you doing here?"

"But, as you can see... I'm a doctor."

"You, a doctor! Since when?"

"Since... My word, since that day we last saw each other, the morning I passed my exam... I'll explain everything, but first let's take a look at that foot."

Boisflambard a doctor! I couldn't believe it, and was even—shall I admit it?—a bit wary of entrusting him with one of my members, even inferior.

"Will you finally explain?" I asked him, once

we were alone.

"My God, it's quite simple. When you knew me in the Latin Quarter, I was in medical school..."

"You never told us."

"You never asked... So, I passed my exams, got my degree, and moved out here, where I made a very nice marriage."

"But, you scoundrel, at what moment of the day did you study the art of curing your fellow man?"

"A few days before my exam, I worked my head off with an old doctor who specialized in that, and besides... besides... I had discovered a trick to pass the test."

"A trick?"

"A marvelous trick, old man, simple and human. Listen to this..."

"For the first exam that I took at medical school, I arrived well turned out, dressed to the nines, resplendent! I need hardly mention that I didn't know the first words of the course. The first man who interviewed me was a professor of natural history. He asked me to describe... and he uttered a word that had never resonated in my ears. I had him repeat his damned word, with no more success for my recollections. Was it animal, vegetable, or mineral? My word, I picked the middle choice, and said:

"'It's a plant...'

"'You didn't hear me, my friend,' the professor continued gently. 'I asked you about...'

"And still that same damned word. So I opted for animal, and, upon signs of impatience from my interrogator, firmly declared that it was a pebble. No luck, really: the professor of natural history also taught physics, and that terrible word that I didn't know was *Ohm's Law*. Need I add that I was pitilessly *flunked*?...

"At the same time as me, there was a poor devil as pitifully attired as I was well dressed. From a scientific point of view, he was approximately my equal. Well, him they passed! I attributed my failure and his success to our different outfits. The examiners had taken pity on the poor young man. They had considered, perhaps, his parents, impoverished, bleeding themselves dry to pay for their son's studies in Paris. A failure meant lost time, more heavy expenses, more and more money lost. Obviously, kind and charitable thoughts had come to them, to those examiners, who are only human, after all, and that was why the poor wretch passed, while I, the son of a good family, was invited to come back the next semester.

"The lesson, as you might guess, was not lost on me. I assembled, with tact, with care, with a skill you can hardly imagine, a more than modest wardrobe, which I wore only for exams: the exact outfit you saw on the last day I wore it, the day I got my diploma. You may not believe me, but

I saw an old hardboiled professor wipe away a tear at the sight of my pathetic getup. He would have whitewashed his blackball for my sake, rather than refuse me, that excellent man."

"That's all very nice," I objected, "but it's not by slipping on an old frock coat, every year in July, that one learns to cure all the diseases that afflict humanity."

"Medicine, old man, is not about science: it's about luck. So, I've often happened to make diagnostic mistakes: even, you know, mistakes that would kill a herd of rhinoceroses. Well! Those were the very cases that brought me cures that my colleagues themselves don't hesitate to call miraculous."

No Consistency in His Ideas

I

He met her in the street one day, and followed her home. Respectfully, at a distance.

Although he was neither timid nor awkward, the young lady seemed so virtuous, so peacefully chaste, that it would have been a crime to disturb, even superficially, such lovely tranquility!

And it was indeed unfortunate, for he couldn't remember ever meeting a prettier girl, he who had seen so many, and loved so many.

A girl or a young woman, it was hard to say, but, in any case, an adorable creature.

A very simple woolen dress clung to her young and supple figure.

A veil clouded her features, which seemed delicate and distinguished.

Between the top of her collar and the bottom of her veil appeared a bit of her neck, just a little bit.

And this glimpse of her white skin, so fresh, gave the young man an intense longing to find out if the rest was consistent.

He didn't dare.

Slowly, and not without majesty, she returned home.

He remained on the sidewalk, more troubled than he cared to admit.

"Good heavens!" he cried. "What a beauty!"

He suppressed a sigh:

"What a pity that she's a virtuous woman!"

He indulged himself by watching her, the next day and the days after that.

He followed her for a long time, with increasing admiration, and with a respect that never faltered.

And every time, when she returned home, he stayed on the sidewalk, stupidly, and murmured:

"What a pity that she's a virtuous woman!"

II

Around the middle of last April, he stopped seeing her.

"Well!" he said to himself. "She must have moved."

"So much the better," he added. "I was becoming seriously infatuated."

"So much the better," he repeated, by way of conclusion.

And yet, the image of the lovely young person never vanished completely from his heart.

Especially that little bit of her neck, next to her ear, that he glimpsed between the top of her collar and the bottom of her veil, insisted on trotting through his brain.

Twenty times, he planned to learn her new address.

Twenty times, a hundred sou coin in his hand, he approached her former building, to interrogate the concierge.

But at the last moment, he turned away and left, replacing the seductive coin in his pocket.

Chance, that great concierge, took it upon herself to reunite these two creatures, the young man who was so amorous and the young lady who was so pure.

But alas! The young lady who was so pure was no longer pure at all.

She had become a cocotte.

And still pretty, for all that!

Much prettier than before, even!

And so bold!

It was at the Eden.

She walked all evening, and walked on disdainful of appearances.

He followed her as before, admiring and respectful.

On several occasions, she drank champagne with various gentlemen.

He waited at a nearby table.

But it was champagne without consequence.

For, a little before the end of the show, she left alone and returned home alone, on foot, slowly, as before, and not without dignity.

When the door of her house closed, he remained stupidly on the sidewalk.

He suppressed a sigh and murmured:

"What a pity she's a whore!"

The Height of Darwinism

I have not always been the doddering, coughing old codger you know today, young readers.

There was a time when I scintillated with grace and beauty.

All the demoiselles would cry, when they saw me pass, "Oh, that charming boy! And how *respectable* he must be!", in which the demoiselles were strangely mistaken, for I was never *respectable*, even in the remotest past of my early youth.

At that time, the muse of Prose had only lightly brushed, with the tip of her vague wing, my ivory brow.

Besides, the nature of my occupations was not conducive to airy fantasies.

I prepared myself, by a course of practice in the best houses of Paris, for the exercise of that deplorable profession that brought fame to M. Fleurant, in the seventeenth century, and to the mischievous Fenayrou, in our own times.

Need I add that the sole fact of my entering a pharmacy resulted in the most imminent and irremediable catastrophes?

My employers quickly became astonished, then worried,

and finally insane, occasionally demented.

As for the clientele, the greater part were felled by sudden death; the others, expressing vehement mistrust, took their business elsewhere.

In short, I harbored in the folds of my waistcoat the specter of bankruptcy, bankruptcy with its green smile.

I possessed an appalling skepticism toward toxic substances; I had an instinctive horror of centigrams and milligrams, which I found so contemptible! Ah, speak to me of grams!

And it often happened that I added copious amounts of the most fearsome poisons to preparations that were previously considered perfectly anodyne.

I especially liked making widows: my own idea.

As soon as a rather nice client appeared at the dispensary, bearing a prescription:

"Who is ill in your household, madame?"

"It's my husband, sir... Oh, it's not serious... A little cold."

So, I said to myself, "Ah, your husband has a cold, does he? Well then! I'll be sure to make his organs pure again." And it was unusual, two days later, not to meet a funeral in the neighborhood.

Those were the good old days!

In the pharmacy in which I found myself sometime

around then, I was gifted with a superior who could have given pointers to Madame Benoîton. Always out.

I liked it that way, having never been keen on incessant surveillance.

Every day, in the afternoon, a sort of old fool, a wealthy man from the neighborhood, an enemy of progress, a clerical obsessive, came to chew his interminable fat with me, in which Darwin was the principal subject.

My old fool considered Darwin a great criminal, and spoke of nothing less than hanging him. (Darwin was not yet dead, at the moment.)

Me, I replied that Bossuet was a clown, and that if I knew where to find his tomb, I would defile it with excrement.

And whole afternoons passed discussing adaptation, selection, transformism, heredity.

"You can say what you like," cried the old fool, "but it's Providence that creates such and such an organ for such and such a function!"

"That's not true," I replied passionately. "Your Providence is a big fat turkey. It's the environment that transforms the organ, and adapts it to its function."

"Your Darwin is a scoundrel!"

"Your Fénelon is a monkey!"

During our pseudo-scientific discussions, you can imagine how conscientiously the prescriptions were prepared.

I remember in particular one poor gentleman who arrived at the most heated moment, with a prescription for two medicines: first, some sort of lotion for his scalp; second, a syrup to purify his blood.

A week later, the poor man returned with his prescription and his empty bottles.

"I feel much better," he said, "but Good Lord! It's appalling how sticky that filthy stuff makes my hair! And it's ruining my hats!"

I glanced at the bottles.

Horrors! I had put the wrong labels on them.

The poor fellow had drunk the lotion, and had conscientiously massaged his scalp with the syrup.

"My word," I said to myself, "since it works for him, we might as well continue."

I learned later that the poor man, who had a supposedly incurable scalp disease, was radically cured after a month of this backward treatment.

(I submit the case to the Academy of Medicine.)

The old fool mentioned above possessed a pure white sheepdog, of which he was very proud, and which he called *Black*, probably because it's the English word for the color that he was not.

One fine day, Black developed an itch, and the old fool asked me what he could do about this inconvenience.

I suggested a sulphur bath.

In fact, there was a veterinarian in the neighborhood who, one day a week, administered a collective sulphur bath to his customers' dogs.

The old fool conducted Black to the bath, and then took a walk during the operation.

When he returned, no more Black.

But a superb black sheepdog, the same size and shape as Black, insisted on licking his hands with an anxious air.

The old fool cried, "Leave me alone, you filthy beast! Black, Black, psst!"

It was, in fact, Black, but blackened; how?

The veterinarian knew nothing about it.

It wasn't the bath, since the other dogs kept their natural color. What, then?

The old fool came to consult me.

I seemed to think for a moment, then suddenly, as if inspired:

"Will you now," I cried, "deny Darwin's theory? Animals adapt not only to their functions, but to their names. You baptized your dog Black, and it was ineluctable that he become black."

The old fool asked if, by chance, I was making fun of him, and left without waiting for an answer.

I can tell you, all of you, how it happened.

The morning of the day that Black was scheduled for his bath, I lured the faithful animal into the laboratory, and thoroughly doused him with lead acetate.

Now, you know that the combination of lead salt and sulphur results in the formation of lead sulphide, a substance blacker than Taupin's mines.

I never saw the old fool again, but, to my great joy, I never ceased noticing Black in the neighborhood.

From the beautiful black due to my chemistry, his coat turned to dirty gray, then to dingy white, and it was a long time before it recovered its immaculate alabaster.

To Set His Mind at Ease

They went out, both of them, heading up the avenue de l'Opéra.

He, an unexceptional dandy, with high, flat, pointed shoes, in tight clothes, as if he'd had to whine to obtain them; in a word, one of our joyful nonentities.

She, much better, petite, as cute as anything, with mad curls all over her forehead, but especially such a waist...

Unbelievable, that waist!

She could have certainly, that little blonde, worn her solid gold luck charm as a belt.

And they headed up the avenue de l'Opéra, he with the flat stupid gait of the dimwitted dandy, she, trotting briskly, carrying her impudent little head high.

Behind them, a tall cuirassier who couldn't believe his eyes.

Completely mesmerized by the phenomenal narrowness of the Parisienne's waist, which he compared, in his mind, to his own plump girlfriend's figure, he murmured to himself:

"It must be fake."

A ridiculous supposition, for anyone who has studied even a little anatomy.

One can have, of course, false teeth, artificial hair, padded hips and breasts, but it's easy to understand that one cannot, in any way, have a fake waist.

But the cuirassier, who incidentally was only second class, was as little informed about anatomy as he was about the artifices of a lady's toilette, and he continued to murmur, quite bewildered:

"It must be fake."

They arrived at the boulevards.

The couple turned right, and, even though he wasn't going that way, the cuirassier followed them.

Decidedly, no, it wasn't possible, it wasn't a real waist. In vain did the tall cavalier recall the loveliest ladies from his hometown, not a one resembled, even from afar, the extraordinary narrowness of that pretty little wasp.

Quite troubled, the cuirassier decided to set his mind at ease, and murmured:

"We'll see if it's fake."

Then, coming two steps to the woman's right, he unsheathed.

The large saber, horizontally, whipped through the air, and cleanly sliced the woman into two pieces, which rolled onto the sidewalk.

Like an earthworm cut by a cruel gardener's spade.

And you should have seen the dandy's face!

The Palm Tree

My mistress, at the moment, is the wife of the baker at the corner of the faubourg Montmartre and the rue de Mauberge.

A fine lad, that tradesman! Gentle and obliging as no other.

When he travels by train, and they come to a steep incline, he leaves his car and runs after the train until the top of the hill:

"That relieves the locomotive," he says, with his sweet smile.

We did our month of military training together, and our relations date from that period of instruction.

He had nothing more urgent, once he was back home, than to introduce me to his wife.

What had to happen happened: his wife adored me and I was crazy about his wife.

(Contrary to the esthetics of delicate folk, I prefer the wives of friends; that way, you know who you're dealing with.)

You all know her, O Parisians of Montmartre (I don't care about the others)! A thousand times, returning to the Butte, you have contemplated her, enthroned behind her counter, amidst the uncountable gold of her bread, under the eternal azure of her ceiling, where the swallows stray.

Her pretty little head, with the hair done like the Virgin, looks rather odd with her overly buxom figure: but me, I like it.

Morally, Marie (for she was called Marie, like you or I) presented a singular mixture of frankness and vice, of ignorance and Machiavellianism.

As innocent as a worm, and as cunning as a ball of twine.

In addition, very generous, but putting into her gifts a delicacy all her own.

"What? You have no watch?" she asked me one day. "Give me thirty francs, and I'll go buy you one from a little watchmaker I know."

And, the next day, she brought me a superb chronometer of some metal that seemed to be gold, with a chain as heavy as the transatlantic cable.

"And how much was this?"

"Twenty-eight francs, dear."

"Twenty-eight francs!?!?"

"Why, yes, dear; he's a little watchmaker in a room... You understand, he doesn't have as many expenses as the big department stores, so..."

"That's fine, it's really not expensive."

She insisted on returning the two francs that she owed me.

Several days later, entirely devoid of resources, I brought my watch to the rue Buffault (the shop that has that filthy flag in front), hoping to get around a hundred sous.

The man weighed the object and asked me timidly if three hundred francs would be enough.

Without moving a muscle in my face, I acquiesced.

But that evening, I could not help gently scolding Marie for her extravagance.

Another time, she arrived all out of breath, flung her arms about me, kissed me over and over, and said:

"Look out the window at the pretty little present that I brought my sweetheart."

In the street, men lifted from a truck a palm tree that seemed somewhat oversized.

"Huh!" she said. "I'm sure you've always wanted a palm tree in your apartment."

I was not mistaken: the palm tree, including the pot, measured no less than 4.20 meters, while my ceiling was no further from my floor than 3.15 meters.

"And besides, you know," she added, "I consider this palm tree a symbol of our love. As long as it's green, you love me. If the leaves turn yellow, it means you're unfaithful."

"But..."

"No buts!"

Nothing was stranger than that poor palm tree, forced, to fit into my apartment, to assume an oblique position. One would have thought some simoon was eternally bending the poor plant.

One day, returning to Paris after an absence of several weeks, I stopped at the bakery before heading for my apartment. Marie was alone.

"Go home now... you'll see the pretty little surprise I got for you."

I entered my domicile, vaguely nervous about the pretty little surprise.

Marie had rented the apartment on the floor above, and cut a circular hole in the floor, through which the top of the famous palm tree could pass in comfort.

An elegant little balustrade surrounded the orifice.

All this work, needless to say, had been accomplished without the concierge or the landlord getting the slightest wind of it.

Several days later, returning home unexpectedly, I found, relatively undressed, Marie and a tall unwashed Egyptian, whom I recognized as a mule driver from the rue de Caire.[1]

Marie was unperturbed.

"This gentleman," she said, indicating the dirty Oriental, "is a gardener in his native land. I invited him to take a look at our palm tree, so he could give us advice on how to care for it."

I politely invited the son of the Pyramids to go tend monocotyledons in other climes.

I glared at the unfaithful woman in mute reproach.

"Don't you believe me, dear?"

"..."

"And yet that's how it is... And besides, you irritate me with your constant jealousy."

And packing her kit, not to mention her caboodle, Marie left.

I was greatly saddened by this separation.

In an attempt to forget her infidelities, I lived it up. You saw nobody but me at the Folies-Bergère, at the Folies-Hippiques, and at other follies, and in all the wild places where you meet those creatures whose bodies are their profession.

Every evening, I went home with a new creature, and loved Marie more than ever.

During this time, the palm tree became superb, sending out new shoots and flourishing as if in the Orient.

One morning, I met Marie when she was out shopping on the faubourg Montmartre. We made up.

She asked about her palm tree.

"Come see for yourself," I said.

She was, in fact, amazed to see it doing so well, but a

bitter thought clouded her pleasure.

"My word!" she said in her most casual tone. "It's not surprising. All those dried up whores you brought here, when I was gone, reminded it of the desert, and it was happy."

I closed her mouth with a kiss behind her ear.

---

1. This story took place during the Universal Exposition of 1889.

The Circumspect Criminal

With an implement (of American manufacture) much like the one used to open canned foodstuffs, the criminal made, in the sheet metal on the front of the shop, two incisions, one vertical, the other horizontal, proceeding from the same point.

With one vigorous movement, he pulled toward himself the triangle of metal thus created, twisting it as easily as a sheet of tinfoil.

(He was a robust criminal.)

He made his way into the little rectangular vestibule that preceded the door.

Holding the glass in place with a rubber suction cup (of American manufacture), he cut it with the help of a diamond from the Cape.

Nothing else prevented his entrance into the shop. Then, calmly, methodically, he piled into a sack *ad hoc* all the precious stones and jewelry, which combined the merit of small volume with the advantage of great value.

He had almost completed his task, when, from the back of the boutique, the owner, M. Josse, made his appearance, a candle in one hand, a revolver in the other.

Very politely, the criminal tipped his hat, and, in a

friendly tone:

"I didn't want," he said, "to pass by without saying hello."

And as, unsuspectingly, the jeweler shook his hand, the criminal plunged into his breast a homicidal blade (of American manufacture).

The sack *ad hoc* was rapidly filled.

The criminal was about to return to the street, when a thought struck him.

Seated on the counter, he traced upon a large sheet of paper a few words in big letters.

With the help of a few sealing wafers, he fastened this placard to the front of the shop, which early morning passersby could read at dawn:

Closed because of death.

The Kisser

The principal occupation between meals, for my friend Vincent Desflemmes, consisted in long wanderings through the streets, through the boulevards, through the quays, and more generally throughout all the arteries of the capital.

Arms swinging freely, unless his hands were in his pockets, Desflemmes went off, without cane, without dog, without woman.

Attentive to the thousand little episodes in the street, Vincent enjoyed them all: disrespectful exchanges between rude coachmen, drunken slaves followed by a cloud of little shouting brats, interrupted pickpockets, bourgeois weddings with the young blushing bride, the dandified groom, the sanguine papa, the fat mama in black silk, the heliotrope maid of honor, the best man ill at ease in his unfamiliar frock coat, the soldier (never a wedding in Paris without a soldier, sometimes a corporal).

The top hats of bourgeois weddings held no more mystery for Vincennes. Little hats with big brims, big hats with little brims, truncated cones, cylinders, hyperboloids, he knew them all, and thus found himself the only man in France able to write a serious essay on *The Top Hat*

Throughout the Ages.

Desflemmes adored weddings; he followed them to the church, entered the holy place, even introduced himself into the sacristy and witnessed, unnoticed in the hubbub, those little comico-touching scenes that are the prerogative of nuptial ceremonies.

By dint of attending this orgy of marriages, Vincent finally noticed a gentleman as fond as he of hymeneal celebrations: a gentleman who was none too handsome, my word, with ugly eyes, a dirty mouth, and a nose that was superabundantly eczematous.

This gentleman must have had countless relatives, for Desflemmes met him everywhere, distributing handshakes, and never forgetting to kiss the bride.

"Who the devil is he, that guy?" Vincent monologized. "In any case, he has a nasty mug."

(My friend Desflemmes didn't put on gloves to talk to himself.)

One fine day, chance informed him about the gentleman with the relatives. The beadle of Saint-Germain-des-Prés was chatting with the deacon.

"Did you see?" asked the beadle. "He was here..."

"Who?" asked the deacon.

"The *kisser.*"

"Ah!"

"Yes... Look, you can see him over there, in the choir, to

the right."

Vincent looked in the direction indicated: the *kisser* was his man.

Quite obligingly, and upon the discreet passage of a forty sou coin, the beadle added to his information.

The *kisser* was a maniac, relatively inoffensive, whose weakness consisted of kissing as many brides in white as possible. Armed with imperturbable aplomb, the *kisser* insinuated himself into the sacristy. The groom's family thought, "He must be some friend of her family." The bride's family came to a parallel conclusion. The *kisser* shook the young man's hand, kissed the bride, and the trick was played.

Desflemmes was quite amused by this strange mania, but swore to himself, if he ever married, to never let the virginal cheeks of his beloved be brushed by such an unpleasant piehole.

A few days after that, Vincent fell madly in love with a young woman from Fontenay-aux-Roses. Although her dowry was negligible, he lost no time in seeking her hand. Besides, there were prospects, a very wealthy uncle, among others, a former lawyer, named N. Hervé (from Jumièges).

"Congratulations!" I said to Desflemmes, who told me the important news. "And the little lady... nice?"

"You have no idea, old man! Oh yes, she's nice! And

funny too! Imagine a forehead and eyes like one of Botticelli's virgins, a witty little nose, a good guy, fun-loving. Madonna and marmoset combined! And in addition, on her cheek, there, by her chin, a beauty mark that sports a few fine hairs, long, curly, and which gives her a thoroughly amusing resemblance to Simili-Meyer. In short, when I saw her, my heart, that old musty powder keg, went off like a fresh stick of dynamite."

The big day arrived.

The uncle with the fortune, N. Hervé (of Jumièges), apologized by telegram for not being able to attend the civil ceremony. No sense waiting for him, he'd go straight to the church.

The nuptial benediction came to a close. The worthy priest pronounced the words that joined the couple before God, as the mayor (or his deputy) had pronounced the words that had joined them before the law.

At that moment, prompted by a mechanical impulse, Desflemmes turned around.

His face passed rapidly from the brick red of anger, to the pale white of suffocation, and finally to the unripe-green-apple of manly resolution.

Behind him, in the last row of the audience, who had Desflemmes just recognized?

Don't look surprised, you've already guessed: the *kisser*!

They were about to proceed into the sacristy.

After asking his young wife to excuse him for a moment, Vincent headed straight for the maniac.

"You," he said, with no apparent affability, "if you don't want to leave the church with a few swift kicks in the pants, you have just one option: back out of here, as soon as possible."

"But, sir..."

"Unless you want me to take you by the scruff of the neck..."

"But, sir..."

"You old pig!"

"But, sir..."

"What is it, you filthy swine, the rest of Paris isn't enough for you?"

As you may well imagine, this interlude had not passed unnoticed among the guests.

"What's wrong?" sighed the worried little Simili-Meyer.

"I don't know," the mama answered, "but your husband seems to be having quite an argument with your Uncle Hervé."

Meanwhile, the discussion continued in the same vein in which it had begun.

Suddenly, Vincent seized Uncle Hervé, for that was indeed who it was, by the arm, and dragged him to the door, with the energetic application of several kicks in the derriere.

"Vincent has gone mad!" cried the bride, collapsing into her armchair.

And all the guests repeated: "Vincent has gone mad!"

Vincent had not gone mad, but on learning the *kisser*'s name, he became quite embarrassed.

With charming philosophy, he took his hat, his coat, and the first train for Paris.

A few days after this regrettable scene, he received news from Fontenay in the form of a request for divorce.

Vincent Desflemmes didn't even hire an attorney. The lawyer for the opposing side had a fine time demonstrating his sudden madness, his incoercible dementia, his disgusting insanity, his frightening alienation. The divorce was granted.

Vincent was free to resume his occupations, which consisted of wandering, between meals, all alone, without cane, without dog, without woman.

He kept a lively penchant for the weddings of others, but never met the *kisser* again.

The Benevolent Suicide

As far back as he could remember, he couldn't recall a single minute of luck throughout all of his poor life. Misfortune, always misfortune! And yet, funny thing, never had this obstinately dark chain of events caused the slightest tinge of rancor or jealousy in him.

He loved his neighbor, and sincerely regretted the grim existence that had been his lot.

One fine day, or rather, one very ugly day, he had had enough of this life, which was really just too stupid.

Calmly, without rhetoric, without posthumous correspondence, without melodramatic posturing, he decided to die. Not to kill himself, but quite simply to stop living, because living without enjoyment seemed flagrantly useless.

The different types of death paraded through his imagination, lugubrious and indifferent.

Drowning, pistol shot, hanging...

He paused at this last method of suicide.

Then, at the moment of death, he was overcome with an immense pity for those who would continue to live after him...

An immense pity and a keen desire to help them.

So, he disappeared into the countryside, and found a field of colza, surrounded by tall poplars.

On the tallest of those poplars, he chose the highest branch.

With the agility of a wild cat—misfortune had not diminished his vigor—he climbed up to it, attached a long rope, what a long rope! and hung himself.

His feet almost touched the ground.

And the next day, when they cut him down before the mayor, an incredible number of people could, in accordance with his last wish, share the interminable rope, and it was for all of them an infinite source of dependable luck.

Esthetic

A few years ago, the aedileship of Pigtown (Ohio, U.S.A.) had the idea of organizing an exhibition of painting, sculpture, engraving, and, in general, everything that follows.

They sent, throughout free America, invitations to artists of both sexes, and constructed, in less time than it takes to write it, a vast hall, next to which the Gallery of Machines would look like a humble attic.

The number of responses surpassed the most optimistic expectations. Everyone with a name in American art wanted to be part of the Pigtown Exhibition.

Several painters and sculptors from the old continent announced their contributions by cable; but the aedileship of Pigtown had decided that the Exhibition was only for Americans ("exclusively national"); they didn't even respond to those European fops.

The Pigtown National Picture and Sculpture Exhibition was an immediate and prodigious success.

The vast hall was never empty, and soon the organizers collected more dollars than they knew what to do with.

Besides, the thing itself was worth the trouble; the sculptures, especially, proved highly interesting to the public.

As far as statues are concerned, the Americans long ago abandoned the outmoded dithering of old Europe. No more of those inanimate groups! Enough of that cold unfeeling marble! Away with those bronze lions devouring ostriches of the same metal, without the ostriches losing a single feather!

American sculptors understand that in Art, only Life matters, and there can be no Life without Movement.

Thus, in the Pigtown exhibition, the statues and sculptures, and even the busts, were all animated. Nostrils flared, breasts heaved, and when a sculpture showed a *Boa Devouring an Ox*, you waited only five minutes before the masterful work, and the ox was effectively devoured by the boa.

The ox was of gutta-percha and the boa of celluloid, you say; O what a tired old complaint! What does the material matter, the idea is all!

In this accumulation of animated art, two works particularly vied for the public's enthusiasm.

The first, due to the inventive genius of the great animal artist K. W. Merrycalf, represented a *Pig Teased by Flies*.

And it was hard to decide which to admire more in this gracious ensemble: The pig? The flies?

The pig, a bronze pig, thirty-six times larger than life, wallowed in a dunghill, also thirty-six times larger than life. A swarm of flies, in the same proportion, frolicked, the little madcaps, around the monstrous snout.

The pig, like all self-respecting pigs, was immobile, but the flies, activated by the most ingenious little mechanism (patent pending), really flew, swirled around, and touched the pig's head only to recharge their batteries and to fly off anew.

It was charming.

This pretty work would have certainly been the hit of the National Exhibition, without the contribution of a previously unknown sculptor, bearing the name of Julius Blagsmith.

Julius Blagsmith's group bore this name in the catalogue: *The Death of the Brave General George-Ern. Baker.* The intrepid officer was depicted at the very moment when, struck in the heart with a bullet, he collapsed onto a nearby machine gun.

To the historic interest of this moving episode was added the ingenious use of the phonograph.

A machine had been skillfully placed inside George-Ern. Baker, and every five minutes, the valiant general, his hand on his heart, cried (in American, of course): "I die for the principle!"

The machine gun, in particular, earned universal acclaim from gunsmiths and sharpshooters. Not a screw, not a bolt, not a rivet, was absent or out of place. A marvel.

It could truly be said: he was so lifelike he could almost talk.

From the first days of the Exhibition, there was one cry from the artistic clans. The first prize in sculpture should go to Merrycalf's *Pig*, unless it went to Blagsmith's *Baker*.

As for the two artists, they conceived a violent dislike for each other. They greeted one another, shook hands, asked after their respective healths, but it was obvious that these courteous relations concealed a polar glaciality.

The morning of the day on which the jury was to announce the awards, Blagsmith politely invited his colleague Merrycalf to a few minutes of conversation. He led him before his sculpture.

"Frankly," he asked, "what do you think?"

"Truthfully," Merrycalf replied, "I think it's perfect. The machine gun is rendered so accurately!..."

"There's no merit in the accuracy of the machine gun, since it's a real machine gun. Take a look."

And Blagsmith, lightly scratching the plaster with his pocket knife, revealed the shiny steel beneath: steel that was, you know, no laughing matter.

"Yes," he continued, "this is a real machine gun, in

perfect condition, with the aggravating circumstance that it's loaded and ready to fire."

"Damn!... and to what end?"

"To the very simple end of shooting all of you, if I don't win the grand certificate of honor."

"You don't beat around the bush, do you!"

"Never! I go straight to it."

"At least give me time to warn the jury."

"As you like."

And, shedding his jacket, Blagsmith adopted the comfortable costume known as "in his shirtsleeves."

Upon a splendid dais draped in plush and adorned with tropical plants, the jury convened.

After an impressive piece performed by the Slaughterhouse Philharmonic of Pigtown, the president of the jury arose and announced the names of the fortunate winners.

He began with painting. Except for a few pistol shots exchanged between the *honorable mention* and the *silver medal*, the announcement of the winners in painting passed without incident. Then, the president announced: "In sculpture, the grand certificate of honor is awarded to Mathias Moonman, creator of..."

Creator of what? I couldn't tell you; for at that precise moment, chaos erupted among the gentlemen who adorned the dais and those around it.

If a thousand million devils vigorously ripped a thousand million bolts of strong canvas, the noise would have been no more infernal, as the murderous projectiles sowed fear and death among the jury and the public.

The dais soon became no more than a confused heap of red drapery, green plants, and jury members of all colors.

Over there, in the back, Blagsmith turned the crank with as much serenity as if he were playing "Yankee Doodle" on a barrel organ.

When he ran out of bullets, he pulled more from the base of his statue and calmly continued his work of destruction.

As everything must end, even the most amusing pranks, the provisions were at last exhausted. Need I add that the public had not hesitated to desert the vast hall? Having come from dust, plaster and marble returned to dust. Only the bronzes escaped with a few negligible dents.

It was over.

Blagsmith slipped on his jacket, as radiant as any gentleman who hasn't wasted his day, when, to his great surprise, he saw coming toward him, who? His rival, Merrycalf.

Merrycalf, affable, all smiles, held out his hand.

"Hurrah, old man! You're a man of your word... and of action."

"You didn't warn the jury, then?"

"Not on your life. It's more fun this way."

"And you? Where were you, during my salvos?"

"In my pig, for goodness sake! You can well imagine that I didn't make a pig thirty-six times larger than life out of solid bronze. I installed a very comfortable little niche inside it, and I can assure you that I wasn't bored there, just now, during your little artillery session."

"Which proves that, as the French say, in the pig everything is good, even the insides."

"Especially when it's hollow."

Delighted with this excellent sally, Blagsmith and Merrycalf went off to dinner with an appetite that bordered on voracity.

A Thoroughly Parisian Drama

CHAPTER I

In which we meet a Lady and Gentleman who would have been happy, but for their constant misunderstandings.

> *O, he chose right well, that customer!*
> RABELAIS.

In the era in which our story opens, Raoul and Marguerite (a pretty name for love) had been married for about five months.

Marriage of inclination, of course.

Raoul, one fine day, on hearing Marguerite sing the pretty ballad by Colonel Henry d'Erville:

The rain, which keeps the frogs alert,
Perfumes and wakes the sleepy wood.
The wood, like Nini, smells so good
When it gets rid of all the dirt.

Raoul, I say, swore that the divine Marguerite (*diva Margarita*) would never belong to any man but himself.

Their household would have been the happiest of

households, except for the foul tempers of the two spouses.

For a yes, for a no, bang! a plate broken, a slap, a kick in the ass.

Hearing these noises, Love fled, weeping, to await, in some hidden nook in the park, the always imminent hour of reconciliation.

Then, countless kisses, endless caresses, tender and expert, the fires of hell.

One might almost believe that the little swine only quarreled for the chance to make up.

CHAPTER II

A simple episode which, although not directly relevant to the plot, will give the clientele an idea of how our heroes lived.

> *In Latin love is called amor,*
> *And bites us mordantly before*
> *It make us mortal, and of course,*
> *Brings tears, traps, forfeits, and remorse...*

(Blazon of love)

One day, however, was worse than usual.

One evening, rather.

−98−

They had gone to the Application Theater, where there was a performance of, among other plays, *The Unfaithful Wife*, by M. de Porto-Riche.

"When you've ogled Grosclaude enough," grumbled Raoul, "let me know."

"And you," vituperated Marguerite, "when you know Mademoiselle Moreno by heart, pass me the opera glasses."

Having begun in this tone, the conversation could only end with the most regrettable reciprocal violence.

In the coupé which took them home, Marguerite took great pleasure in scratching away at Raoul's self-esteem, as if on an old and broken mandolin.

Once home, the opponents assumed their respective positions.

Hand raised, eye fierce, mustache bristling like a wildcat's, Raoul advanced on Marguerite, who, at that point, began to wax sore afraid.

The poor creature fled, furtive and fleet, like a doe in the great forest.

Raoul was about to catch her.

Then, an inspired flash of supreme anguish illuminated Marguerite's little brain.

Turning suddenly, she threw herself into Raoul's arms, crying:

"Protect me, my little Raoul!"

CHAPTER III

In which our friends reconcile as I hope you often reconcile, you who think you're so clever.

"Hold your tongue, please!"

. . . .
. . . .
. . . .
. . .

CHAPTER IV

In which we observe that people who meddle in things that do not concern them should mind their own business.

"It's amazing how nasty everyone is these days!"

(A remark from my concierge, last Monday morning.)

One morning, Raoul received the following note:

"If you would like, for once, to see your wife in a good mood, go then, Tuesday, to the Incoherents' Ball, at the Moulin Rouge. She will be masked, and disguised as a Congolese pirogue. A word to the wise.
A FRIEND."

The same morning, Marguerite received the following note:

"If you would like, for once, to see your husband in a good mood, go then, Tuesday, to the Incoherents' Ball, at the Moulin Rouge. He will be masked, and disguised as a Templar from the turn of the century. A word to the wise. A FRIEND."

These billets did not fall on deaf ears.

Admirably concealing their plans, when the fatal day arrived:

"My dear," Raoul said, with his most innocent expression, "I will be forced to leave you until tomorrow. Matters of the greatest importance call me to Dunkirk."

"It couldn't come at a better time," Marguerite replied with delicious ingenuousness. "I have just received a telegram from my Aunt Aspasie, who is gravely ill and summons me to her side."

CHAPTER V

In which we see the wild youth of today wallow in the most fleeting and chimerical pleasures, rather than think of eternity.

> *But I still want to live:*
> *Life is so beautiful!*
> AUGUSTE MARIN

The columnists of the *Limping Devil* unanimously proclaimed that the Incoherents' Ball that year was arrayed with unusual brilliance.

Many shoulders and quite a few legs, not counting the accessories.

Two attendees seemed not to partake in the general merriment: a Templar from the turn of the century and a Congolese pirogue, both hermetically masked.

As the clock struck three, the Templar approached the Pirogue and asked her to dine with him.

In answer, the Pirogue lay her little hand on the Templar's robust arm, and the couple departed.

CHAPTER VI

In which the plot thickens.

> *"I say, don't you think the*
> *rajah laughs at us?"*
> *"Perhaps, sir."*
>
> HENRY O'MERCIER

"Leave us for a moment," the Templar told the waiter in the restaurant. "We'll consult the menu and call for you."

The waiter retired, and the Templar carefully locked the door of the room.

Then, with a sudden gesture, after removing his own mask, he tore off the Pirogue's loup.

Both of them, at once, let out a cry of surprise, for neither recognized the other.

He was not Raoul.

She was not Marguerite.

They apologized to one another, and lost no time in becoming better acquainted over a light supper, I need say no more.

CHAPTER VII

A happy ending for everyone, except the others.

> *Let's drink vermouth with grenadine,*
> *The hope of our old battalions.*
> GEORGE AURIOL

This little misadventure taught Raoul and Marguerite a lesson.

From that moment on, they never quarreled again and were perfectly happy.

They have no children yet, but that will come.

Mam'zelle Miss

The oldest of the three, Miss Grace, was an ordinary fat girl, as only the English can be when they decide to be ordinary.

Little Lily, the youngest, looked rather comical with her flaming red hair, but flaming as only English hair can be when it decides to be flaming.

The one I loved the most was the middle one, Miss Emily, whom I called, for my own amusement, Mam'zelle Miss.

At that time, Miss Emily must have been around fifteen, but she was fifteen as only the English can be when they decide to be fifteen.

She went to school with my cousins, and it often happened that, in the evening, I accompanied the girls.

When it came time to separate, they all kissed one another. I, looking as innocent as possible, pretended to be part of the round, and kissed all of that pretty little group.

Mam'zelle Miss sweetly let me, although I was already a big boy. And I remember that the place where I kissed her looked all red on her cheeks, so fine and delicate was her pink skin.

Sometimes I pressed a little too hard, and then she

reproached me, and her native "Britishism" made her reproaches sound like the warbling of a bird.

Whenever she laughed, her upper lip drew back and revealed the humid nacre of her delectable choppers.

It was especially her hair that I loved, hair as fine as hair, and of such light gold that I thought I was dreaming.

Their father, a strikingly handsome man, as handsome as only the English can be when they decide to be handsome, adored his three little ones, and replaced, by dint of his tenderness, their mother, who was long dead.

When I left for Paris, I felt, in addition to the sorrow of quitting my home and my parents, a pang of despair on thinking that I would never see Mam'zelle Miss again, and I never forgot her.

On my first vacation home, the first thing I did was to ask about my little friend.

Alas! How the family had changed!

The father drowned on an ocean voyage. (No trace of his fortune was ever found, and it remained a mystery how he had managed to live, until the present, in relatively considerable affluence.)

Miss Grace left for India, as the governess in a Scottish major's family; Lily was adopted by a minister, who blushed at having only fourteen daughters among his seventeen children.

As for Mam'zelle Miss, I didn't want to believe her

new situation.

And yet it was true.

Mam'zelle Miss, cashier in a butcher's shop.

Twenty times a day, I passed the shop. It was, as it happened, market day.

The store filled unceasingly with peasants, cooks, and women from town.

The busy butcher boys cut, carved off pieces from the big slabs of meat, and delivered the merchandise with commentary that did not always sparkle with good taste. And there were endless discussions about the choice of cuts, the weight, and the bones.

Amid all this brouhaha, Mam'zelle Miss calmly made out vertiginously quick and numerous receipts. Dressed severely in black, a high collar, tight white cuffs, she had, despite her still childish face, the thoroughly amusing air of a reasonable little woman.

From time to time, she interrupted her work to brush away, with a furtive gesture, the curls that flew across her forehead.

At last, she raised her head and glanced absently out at the street.

She saw me rooted there, and stared at me for a few seconds, with that candid yet irritating insolence peculiar to myopic young women.

By her pale smile, I understood that I had been

recognized, and I was instantly happy.

Near the end of my vacation, one day, I didn't see her in the shop.

Nor the next day.

That evening, I questioned a young butcher boy, who told me:

"The boss had long suspected something. The night before last, coming back from the Beaumont market, he went up to his room, and found her in bed with the first boy, both as drunk as skunks. So, he kicked them out."

The Good Painter

He was preoccupied with tonal harmony to such an extent that certain colors, poorly arranged in provincial clothing or on the canvases of members of the Institute, made him gnash his teeth in despair, like a musician faced with discords.

To such an extent that, for nothing in the world, would he ever drink red wine with fried eggs, because it would make an ugly combination in his stomach.

One time when, walking briskly, he jostled a young dandy in a beige overcoat against a freshly painted green storefront (*Warning: Wet Paint*), and the young dandy told him, "Watch where you're going...", he replied, while squinting, as painters do when eyeing a painting:

"What are you complaining about?... It's more Japanese this way."

The other day, he received a postcard from an old comrade who was hunting a black panther for the Great Cats exhibit in Trieste.

He was touched that someone had thought of him, so far away and from so long ago, and he wrote his old comrade a good long letter, a very heavy good letter in a big envelope.

Since Java is far away, and the letter was heavy, the

postage cost him an arm and a leg.

The clerk at the Post Office tendered him, irritably, five or six stamps whose color varied with their prices.

Then, calmly, taking his time, he pasted the stamps onto the big envelope, vertically, taking great care that the various tints harmonized—*so they wouldn't clash.*

Almost satisfied, he went to drop his letter into the yawning slot marked "Foreign," when a last critical look made him precipitously return.

"Another three sou stamp."

"Here, sir."

And he pasted it onto the envelope beneath the others.

"But, sir," the clerk remarked amiably, "your correspondence had enough postage."

"No matter," he said.

Then, complacently:

"It's to call back a bit of blue."

The Zebras

"Would you like to see a truly curious spectacle, and one that you cannot boast of having often contemplated, you who are from this area?"

This proposition was made to me by my friend Sapeck, on the pier in Honfleur, one summer afternoon, about four or five years ago.

Naturally, I accepted at once.

"Where will this extraordinary performance take place," I asked, "and when?"

"Around four or five o'clock, in Villerville, on the road."

"Damn! We don't have much time!"

"We have enough... my car awaits us in front of the White Horse."

And there we were, galloping off behind two little horses harnessed in tandem.

An hour later, all of Villerville, artists, tourists, bourgeois, natives, alerted that something out of the ordinary was about to happen, lined up along the road that leads from Honfleur to Trouville.

The suspense was at the highest point of overexcitement. Sapeck, eagerly questioned, wrapped himself in a mysterious mutism.

"Look!" he suddenly cried. "There's one!"

One what? All eyes turned, anxiously, to the cloud of dust indicated by Sapeck's fatidic finger, and we saw a tilbury appear, driven by a lady and gentleman, which tilbury was pulled by a zebra.

A beautiful tall zebra, well-proportioned, resembling, in its general outlines, a horse more than a mule.

The lady and gentleman in the tilbury didn't seem particularly flattered by the attention. The man muttered some words, probably uncomplimentary, about the populace.

"And there's another!" Sapeck cried.

There was in fact another zebra, harnessed to a carriole stuffed with a little family.

Less elegant in shape than the first, the second zebra, however, honored the reputation for speed honored by its congeners.

The people in the carriole had an almost insolent attitude toward the curious crowd.

"You can tell they're Parisians!" a young country lass cried. "They've never seen anything before!"

"Another one!" shouted Sapeck.

And zebras followed zebras, all different in form and bearing.

Some were as big as big horses, others as small as small asses.

The caravan even included a priest, clinging to a little green car pulled by a very pretty little zebra, which galloped like a fiend.

Our reaction brought up the worthy priest's shoulders, unctuously. His housekeeper called us "a bunch of hooligans."

And then, finally, the road returned to its ordinary physiognomy: the zebras had passed.

"Now," said Sapeck, "I will explain the phenomenon. The people you have just seen are from Grailly-sur-Toucque, and are notorious for their peevish disposition. One can even cite, among them, cases of extraordinary ferocity. Since the most ancient times, they have used, for transport and for working their fields, those zebras of which you have just contemplated a few examples. They have always been protective of their animals, and have always refused to sell a single one to people from other towns. It is supposed that Grailly-sur-Touque is an ancient African colony, brought to Normandy by Julius Caesar. Scholars disagree about this very curious case of ethnography."

The next day, I heard an explanation for the phenomenon which was less ethnographic, but more plausible.

I met good mother Toutain, the hostess at the Siméon farm, where Sapeck was staying.

Mother Toutain was beside herself:

"Ah! He told me a pack of lies, your friend Sapeck! Just

imagine that yesterday we had a lot of people from the parish of Grailly, on pilgrimage to Notre-Dame-de-Grâce. These people put their horses and asses in our stable. Monsieur Sapeck sent all my staff on errands for him in town. Me, I was off at my market. Meanwhile, Monsieur Sapeck borrowed pots of paint from the painters working at Monsieur Dufay's house, and made stripes on all the horses and asses. By the time the Grailly people noticed, the paint was dry. No way of getting it off! Ah, they made such a fuss, those Grailly people! They're threatening to sue me. Oh, that Monsieur Sapeck!"

Sapeck nobly rectified his misdeed, the very next day.

He recruited about ten of those lazy and shabby loafers who are the ornament of every port town.

He piled this lovely bunch into an immense charabanc, with a supply of brushes, currycombs, and several cans of gasoline.

To the sound of a trumpet, he exhorted the inhabitants of Grailly, possessors of provisional zebras, to bring their animals to the village square.

And the shabby loafers began to *dezebrate*.

A few hours later, there were no more zebras in that ancient African colony than there are in the palm of my hand.

I wanted to recount this innocent, true, and amusing prank pulled by poor Sapeck, because he has been saddled with so many others, idiotic ones that he would never have imagined.

And besides, I have no objection to disabusing the few innocent tourists who might still believe that there are herds of zebras in certain parts of the Normandy coast.

Simple Misunderstanding

Angéline (did I tell you her name was Angéline?) bore a striking resemblance to Raphael's *Madonna of the Chair*, without the chair, but with something more reserved in her features.

Tall, blonde, distinguished, and yet Angéline didn't descend from a family catalogued in the Gotha, or even in the Bottin.

Her father, a fine old Badener, my word! municipally swept the streets of Paris (*Fluctuat nec mergitur*). Her mother, a ruddy and stumpy Auvergnate, was attached, in the position of bread porter, to one of the most important bakers on the boulevard de Ménilmontant.

As for Angéline, when I met her, she was exercising her talents with a prestigious milliner on the rue de Charonne.

Her complexion of crushed lilies and roses went straight to my heart.

(I implore my readers not to take those crushed flowers literally. One day last summer, to see for myself, I crushed some lilies and roses in my washbasin. It was revolting! And if you met a woman bearing that particular tint on the street, you wouldn't have enough urban ambulances to rush her to Saint-Louis hospital.)

How did that sweeper and bread basket manage to engender such a prettily delicate object as Angéline! The mysteries of generation!

Perhaps the Auvergnate cuckolded the Badener one day with an English painter?

(English painters, as everyone knows, are renowned throughout the entire universe for their extreme beauty.)

It was indeed time that I took Angéline as my mistress, for the next day she might fall into sin.

Her delight at being released from confecting hats for the fashion plates of the eleventh arrondissement knew no bounds, and she showed me the most flattering affection, affection which I attributed to my charms alone.

I wasted no time (poor fool!) in parading my new conquest before the dazzled eyes of my comrades.

"Charming!" they chorused. "You lucky dog!"

Only one of my friends, the son of a wealthy Amsterdam pharmacist, Van Deyk-Lister, felt compelled to mock me, in his native accent, which aggravated the offense:

"Yes, she's not bad, your little one, but I wouldn't suggest you get used to her."

"Why not?"

"Because I suspect that she won't grow moss in your arms."

"Nonsense! I'll keep her as long as I like!"

"Nonsense yourself! Me, I'll have her whenever I like!"

"Egotist!"

"I'll bet you fifty louis that she'll be my mistress before the end of the year."

(We were then at the beginning of December.)

Fifty louis, that was quite a sum for me, at the time! But what's the risk when one is certain?

I made the bet.

Certain? Yes, I thought I was certain, but with women can one ever be certain? *Donna è mobile.*

I did not neglect reporting Van Deyk-Lister's impertinent remarks to my Angéline.

"Well! He has his nerve, your friend!"

After a pause:

"Fifty louis, how much is that?"

"It makes a thousand francs."

"Golly!"

We never spoke about the ridiculous wager again, but I never stopped thinking about the fifty lovely louis I would finger at the end of the month.

One evening I didn't find Angéline at home. She didn't return until quite late.

More affectionate than usual, she threw her arms around my neck, kissed me in a place she knew quite well, and in her most sirenian voice:

"My dear," she said, "promise you won't be angry with what I have to tell you..."

"That depends."

"No, it doesn't depend! Promise."

"But..."

"No, no buts! Promise."

"I promise."

"Good! Well, you know we're not rich, at the moment..."

"You could say we're in the most viscous of soups."

"Exactly. Well! I thought if you could win fifty louis so easily, it would be stupid to be embarrassed..."

"I don't understand."

"So, I went to see your friend Van Deyk-Lister, and like that, he owes you fifty louis."

Unfortunate woman! That's how she understood bets!

Was it jealousy? Was it anger at losing a thousand francs so stupidly? I don't remember, but the fact remains that at that moment I resembled a bombshell in operation more than a human being endowed with reason.

"So you didn't understand, you stupid cow," I screamed, "that because that filthy Dutchman slept with you, now I'm the one who owes him fifty louis?"

"My God, my God! I'm so stupid!" she burst out sobbing.

And so that she not moan for nothing, I administered a pair of slaps, or two.

There are those whose laughter is hollow: Angéline's weeping was full, for I soon saw shining through the subsiding wave of her tears the rainbow of her smile.

"May I say something, dear?"

"..."

"I have an idea. You'll see, you won't lose your money."

"..."

"Tomorrow I'll go back to Van Deyk-Lister and tell him to keep quiet. That way, he's the one who will owe you fifty louis."

I willingly acquiesced to this ingenious proposition.

(I should add, as an excuse, that these events took place in a year in which, after a fall from a horse, I had lost all moral values.)

Quite faithfully, Van Deyk-Lister, on December 31st, at midnight, handed me the agreed sum.

I pocketed the cash without moving a muscle in my face, and even offered the loser a bock.

Often, after that, Angéline returned to Van Deyk-Lister. Each time, she returned bearing little sums, which, although they didn't amount to a considerable fortune, brought a bit of comfort to our humble household.

The Young Lady and the Old Pig

There was once a young lady of great beauty who was in love with a pig.

Madly!

Not one of those pretty little pigs, pink, mischievous, those little pigs that furnish the trade with such exquisite knuckles of ham.

No.

But an old pig, shabby, all its bristles gone, a pig for which the most depraved butcher in the country would not have given a sou.

A dirty pig, too!

And she loved it... You should have seen her!

For an empire, she would not have consented to leave to her servants the task of preparing its food.

And it was truly charming to see her, this young lady of great beauty, mixing good potato peelings, good bran, good apple parings, good bread crusts.

She rolled back her sleeves and, with her own arms (which were quite pretty), stirred it all into good dishwater.

When she arrived in the courtyard with her bucket, the old pig arose from its dungheap and trotted over on its old feet, emitting grunts of satisfaction.

It plunged its head into its rations and rooted around up to its ears.

And the young lady of great beauty felt flooded with happiness to see it so content.

And then, when it had eaten its fill, it returned to its dungheap, without the slightest look from its dingy little eyes to its benefactress.

What a dirty pig!

Big green flies swooped, buzzing, down on its ears, and feasted, in their turn, in the sunshine.

The young lady, filled with sorrow, returned to her papa's cottage with her bucket empty and tears in her eyes (which were quite pretty).

And the next day, always the same thing.

Now, one day it happened to be the pig's name day.

What the pig's name was, I don't remember, but it was its name day all the same.

All week, the young lady of great beauty had been scratching her head (which was quite pretty) over what fine and agreeable gift she could offer, that day, to her old pig.

She couldn't think of one.

So she said simply, "I'll give it flowers."

And she went down into the garden, which she stripped of its most beautiful plants.

She put armfuls of them in her apron, a pretty apron of purple silk, with such nice little pockets, and took them to the old pig.

And then wasn't the old pig furious, and didn't it grumble like a bear.

What did it care for roses, lilies, and geraniums!

Roses pricked it.

Lilies got yellow all over its snout.

And geraniums gave it a headache.

There were also clematises.

It ate all the clematises, like a glutton.

However little you may have studied the application of botany to nutrition, you must know that if clematises are unhealthy for man, they're fatal to pigs.

The young lady of great beauty was unaware of this.

And yet she was an educated young woman. She even had her diploma.

And the clematises that she offered her pig belonged precisely to that terrible species *Clematis pigicida*.

The old pig died from them, after terrible agonies.

They buried it in a field of colza.

And the young lady stabbed herself on its grave.

Sancta Simplicitas

There are, in this world, complicated people and simple people.

Complicated people can't move their little finger without seeming to set off the most mysterious machinery. The existence of certain complicated people is like a vast intricacy of coiled springs and counterweights.

That's what complicated people are like.

Simple people, on the other hand, say yes when they mean yes, no when they mean no, open their umbrella when it rains (if they have an umbrella), and close it as soon as the rain has ceased to fall. Simple people go straight on their way, unless there's a barricade that compels them to make a detour.

That's what simple people are like.

Among the simplest people I've known, there are three, one of whom entered into relations with the other two under conditions of such simplicity that I request your permission to tell their story, if you have a minute.

The first of these simple people is a young gentleman, a quite handsome and wealthy lad, named Louis de Saint-Baptiste.

The other two were composed of M. Balizard, a

prominent metallurgist in the Haut-Marne, and Mme Balizard, a young woman who was not very pretty, if you please, but irresistible to those who like that type.

One evening, Mme Balizard simply asked her husband:

"Are we going to Paris soon to see the Exposition?"

"Impossible," the metallurgist simply responded. "I have a lot of money at stake now, and I'd be even more foolish than all my foolish furnaces combined, if I left my factory at this moment."

"Fine," Mme Balizard simply replied, "we'll wait."

"But who's stopping you from going alone, if you like?"

"Fine, dear."

And the very next day after this conversation (simplicity does not preclude swiftness) Mme Balizard took the express for Paris, quite simply.

A few days after her arrival, she found herself at the Rumanian Cabaret, genuinely moved by the music of the Lăutari (simplicity does not preclude art), when a tall, very handsome young man sat beside her.

It was Louis de Saint-Baptiste.

He looked at her with a simplicity not devoid of interest.

She looked at him under the same conditions.

And he said:

"Madame, you have exactly the features and attitude that I love in a woman. I would be curious to know if your voice has the timbre that I love as well. Say a few words, if you please."

"Willingly, sir. As for me, I find you very seductive, with your distinguished air, your blue eyes which gaze out on the world like a big baby, and your blond hair, which curls so naturally, and is so fine."

"I'm glad that we like each other. Shall we dine together?"

They dined together that evening, and, the next day, they lunched together.

The day after that, it was not only their meals that they shared.

But all of that, so simply!

The best of things must end, down here on this earth, and soon, Mme Balizard had to return to Saint-Dizier.

Not alone.

God had blessed her fleeting and sinful (socially) union with M. de Saint-Baptiste.

The latter was informed as soon as it was certain, and he shivered with joy in his simple heart.

It was a little girl.

One fine morning the next month, Saint-Baptiste said simply to himself:

"I'll go get my little girl."

And he took the express for Saint-Dizier.

"Monsieur Balizard, please?"

"That is I, sir."

"Me, I'm M. Louis de Saint-Baptiste, and I've come to

take my little girl."

"What little girl?"

"The little girl that Mme Balizard delivered last week."

"She's your daughter?"

"Precisely."

"Well! I'm surprised my wife didn't mentioned it."

"Perhaps it didn't occur to her."

"Probably."

And in a loud voice, M. Balizard cried:

"Marie!"

(Marie was Mme Balizard's name, a simple name.)

Marie arrived and very simply:

"Well," she said, "Louis! How are you?"

But M. Balizard, who was pressed for time, cut short the effusions.

"My dear, M. de Saint-Baptiste claims that he's the father of the baby."

"It's perfectly true, dear; I have special reasons for being sure about it."

"We should give him the child, then... You can take care of that. I beg your pardon for leaving you so abruptly, but a big job supplying the railroad... I'll see you soon, Marie... Your obedient servant, sir."

"Good day, sir."

A Really Good One

Our cousin Rigouillard was what is known as a comical cuss, but because he had a tidy little fortune, the whole family put on a good face for him, despite his eccentric habits.

Where he had accumulated his fortune, that's what no one could explain clearly.

Cousin Rigouillard had left the country, at a young age, and had returned, one fine day, with innumerable parcels containing the most heterogeneous objects, stuffed ostriches, Kanak pirogues, Japanese porcelain, etc.

He bought a house with a little garden, not far from us, and there he grew old peacefully and cheerfully, busying himself with organizing his innumerable collections, and playing a thousand jokes on his neighbors and on others' neighbors.

It was that, above all, that earned him the disapproval of the serious people in the area: a man of his age amusing himself with such childish pranks, was that reasonable?

I, who was not a "serious person" at the time, I adored my old cousin, who seemed to epitomize all modern happiness.

His accounts of the tricks he'd played in his youth plunged me into the most delirious delight, and, although

I knew them all almost by heart, it brought me ever keener pleasure to hear them told and retold.

"And you," my cousin asked me, "did you play any tricks on your prefects today?"

Alas, did I! It was a major preoccupation (I still blush over it), and a day spent without fooling some prefect or teacher seemed, to me, a day wasted.

One day, in history class, the teacher asked me the name of a farmer-general. I pretended to think deeply, and answered with frightening gravity:

"Cincinnatus!"

The whole class doubled over in mad spasms of unconfined hilarity. The teacher alone had not understood. However, light came into his brain at last. He suffered a bout of indignation, and dismissed me *illico*, with a supply of assignments capable of exhausting the brain of the most hardened child.

My cousin Rigouillard, to whom I recounted this adventure the same evening, was enchanted with my behavior, and his approval manifested itself in the immediate gift of a brand new fifty centime coin.

Rigouillard had a passion for archeological collections, but a violent aversion to archeologists, all because his application to the Archeological Society had been rejected by an enormous majority.

They thought he wasn't serious enough.

"Archeology is a fine science," my cousin often told me, "but archeologists are a bunch of pathetic fools."

He reflected a few minutes, and added, rubbing his hands:

"And besides, I have a good one in store for them... a really good one, even!"

And I wondered what really good trick my cousin had in store for the archeologists.

A few years later, I received a letter from my family. My cousin Rigouillard was very ill, and wanted to see me.

I sped to his side.

"Ah, there you are, little one. Thank you for coming; shut the door, for I have something important to say to you."

I bolted the door, and sat by my cousin's bed.

"You're the only one in the family," he continued, "who understands me; and so you're the one that I assign to carry out my final wishes... for I'm going to die soon."

"No, cousin, no..."

"Yes, I know what I'm saying, I'm going to die, but when I die I want to play a trick on the archeologists, a good trick!"

And my cousin gaily rubbed his withered hands.

"When I've snuffed it, put my body in the big suit of Chinese armor in the vestibule below, the one that scared you so much when you were little."

"Yes, cousin."

"Then put the whole business in the stone coffin in the garden... you know, the Gallo-Roman coffin!"

"Yes, cousin."

"And slip beside me this leather purse containing my collection of Greek coins: that's how I want to be buried."

"Yes, cousin."

"In five or six hundred years, when the archeologists dig me up, just imagine their faces, eh? A Chinese warrior with Greek coins in a Gallo-Roman coffin?"

And my cousin, in spite of his illness, laughed to the point of tears, at the idea of the faces the archeologists would make, in five hundred years.

"I'm not curious," he added, "but I'd certainly like to read the report those imbeciles will write about their discovery."

A few days later, my cousin died.

The day after his funeral, we learned that his whole fortune was in an annuity.

That detail helped to soften considerably my remorse at failing to slip into the coffin his collection of Greek coins (mostly gold).

It might as well profit me, I told myself, as some archeologists yet to be born.

Dirty Trick

During the year 187... or 188... (I have no time now to determine exactly this painful era), the Pactolus seldom flooded the modest lodging that I occupied near Luxembourg (the garden, not the grand duchy).

My family (nice people, though), vexed at seeing me not get more brilliant grades (truthfully, they would have been content with dim grades), had cut off my support as with a razor.

And I shivered in need, indigence, and penury.

My sole income (if you can call it an income) consisted in some doggedly zany columns that I wrote for a sort of big lout of a student, who signed his own name to them in the *Left Bank Doodlebug* (an organ now vanished).

The big lout remunerated me with tiny sums, but I revenged myself deliciously for his rapacity by sleeping with his girlfriend, a quite lovely girl whom he later married.

Those were good times.

We had a good appetite, found everything delicious, and were as happy as gods when, in the evening, we managed to swipe a pot of mustard from Canivet, the grocer whose shop was a little past the Saint-Louis school, next to the Sherry-Gobbler.

The only thing that bothered me occasionally was the rent.

And what bothered me about the rent wasn't paying it (I didn't pay it), but precisely not paying it. Do you understand?

Every evening, when I returned, I was stricken with terror at the idea of confronting my concierge's observations, and especially her stare.

Oh, that concierge's stare!

God preserve you forever from a concierge who stares at you as mine stared at me!

That concierge's pupils seemed like a meeting of all the evil stares in creation.

There was, in that stare, hyena, tiger, pig, hooded cobra, fried sole, and slug.

What a nasty old woman!

She was a widow, and nothing could dissuade me from the idea that her husband had perished a victim of the *stare*.

I, who thought myself much too young to die that way, or more generally in any other way, I ruminated a thousand plans for moving.

When I say moving, I flatter myself, for it was a simple escape that I planned, what one might call a discreet getaway.

In that period, my moral fiber was extremely underdeveloped.

Having learned to read Proudhon, I never doubted that property was theft, and the thought of abandoning an apartment, without bothering to settle a few overdue payments, contained nothing to inflict me with the agony of remorse.

My landlord, besides, precluded all ideas of sympathy.

A former bailiff, he had built his great fortune on the disaster and ruin of his contemporaries.

Each floor in his buildings represented at least one bankruptcy, and I was sure that pitiless individual had as much human despair on his conscience as entries in his General Ledger.

The first of July and of October passed without me offering the least sum to my concierge.

Oh, those stares!

I received a few examples of epistolary prose from my landlord, who indicated the first of January as the extreme limit of his indulgence.

It was then that I conceived a plan which, even now, I still consider ingenious.

On January first, I sent my landlord a calling card on which was printed:

Alphonse Allais

MANUFACTURER OF SMASHITE

January 8th came and went, as far as my remittance went, exactly as July 8th and October 8th had gone.

That evening, my concierge's *stare* (oh, that stare!) and the following communication:

"Don't leave too early tomorrow morning. The landlord wants to talk with you."

I didn't leave too early, and was right not to, for if I ever had fun in my life, it was that morning.

I plastered my apartment with enormous signs:

Smoking strictly forbidden

I spread about a pound of starch on an immense sheet of white paper, and awaited developments.

....

Heavy footsteps on the stairs; it's the former bailiff.

The doorbell rings. I open.

As it happens, he has a cigar in his mouth.

I tear the cigar from his mouth and hurl it down the stairs, concealing, beneath my mask of terror, a strong urge to laugh.

"Hey! What are you doing?" he cries in alarm.

"What am I doing?... Can't you read?"

And I show him the *Smoking strictly forbidden.*

"Why is that, smoking forbidden?"

"Because, unfortunate man, if a smidgen of your cigar ash had fallen on this smashite, we would all have exploded, you, me, your building, the whole neighborhood!"

My landlord was not, ordinarily, very colorful, but at that moment his features took on that particular green that is close to dirty violet.

He stuttered, stammering, drooling in fright:

"And... you... make... that... in... my... building!"

"Certainly!" I responded with utter composure. "If you want to buy me a factory in the middle of the deserted moors..."

"Hurry up and get the hell out of here!"

"Not before paying my back rent."

"You can keep it, but, please, get the hell out, you and your..."

"Smashite!... Next to my smashite, sir, dynamite is no more dangerous than roach powder."

"Get the hell out! Get the hell out!"

And I got the hell out.

Anesthetic

Listen to us wax poetic,
Anesthetic, anesthetic,
Etc. (Familiar song.)

The first floor of the sumptuous residence was occupied by a dentist from Toulouse, who had put on his door a brass plate reading: *Surgeon dentist.*

In their ignorance of the English language, the maids of the house had concluded that the Toulousain was named Surgeon, and said, without a single discordant objection being raised: "A handsome guy, huh, that M. Surgeon."

(In case this sheet ever falls under the eyes of a maid of the house, let her know that *surgeon* means *chirurgien* in English.)

The maids of the house were, in this case, expert connoisseurs, for M. Surgeon (let's keep the name) constituted, on his own, one of the most dashing men of these last years of the century.

Imagine the bust of Lucius Verus, completed with the torso of the Farnese Hercules—but more modern, of course.

The second floor of the sumptuous residence in question was occupied by M. Lecoq-Hue and his young wife.

Not very nice, M. Lecoq-Hue. Smallish, thinnish, reddish, his hair sparse, his eye rheumy; no, decidedly, M. Lecoq-Hue was not very nice! And, besides, as jealous as a jungle! The story of his marriage was exceedingly curious, and many novels have been written about less than that.

Very rich, he met a very beautiful young woman, the teacher of his sister-in-law's children. He fell madly in love with this pretty person, obtained her hand, and used the occasion to marry her.

The teacher never forgave him for being so ugly and insufficient. Long before the marriage had been finalized, she had sworn revenge. After the marriage, she renewed her oath, which was fiercer, this time, and better informed.

Not a day passed in which M. Surgeon did not meet the delicious and superb Madame Lecoq-Hue on the stairs.

Every time, he said to himself:

"Wow!... There's a woman you wouldn't get bored with!"

Every time, she said to herself:

"Wow!... There's a man you wouldn't get bored with!"

(I cannot guarantee the exact wording of this double remark, but I can verify its precise spirit.)

They eventually greeted one another, and, shortly afterward, started asking after each other's health.

And then, little by little, they talked about one thing and another, but furtively, alas! and always on the stairs. One day, Surgeon, emboldened, dared to risk:

"What a pity, Madame, that you're such a poor patient of mine!"

A regret mixed with flattery, for, among her other perfections, Madame Lecoq-Hue was endowed with teeth beside which all the dentures on the African coast paled in comparison.

This regret mixed with flattery sparked in Madame Lecoq-Hue's brain the sudden light of a good idea.

The next day, with that natural air all women have when they're up to no good (or to good, for that matter):

"My dear, I'm going down to the dentist."

"To do what, darling?"

"But... to do what you do at the dentist, of course!"

"Do you have a toothache, then?"

"It's driving me mad."

"Mad with love."

"Idiot!"

And, with that conciliatory word, she descended the stairs that separated her from M. Surgeon.

A toothache!... Her! The very idea! M. Lecoq-Hue felt budding in his breast the sting of doubt.

He too knew the handsome Surgeon, the superb Lucius Verus, the disturbing Farnese Hercules on the first floor.

No, a toothache, that wasn't natural. Livid with jealousy, he too rang at the surgeon's door.

It was M. Surgeon himself who answered.

"May I help you, sir?"

Timidity? Shame? Fear of being wrong? I don't know; but M. Lecoq-Hue stammered:

"I came to ask you to extract a tooth."

"Perfectly, sir; sit here, in this chair. Open your mouth. Which one?"

"This one."

"Perfectly... Without or *with* pain?"

And the terrible man pronounced "with," as if this simple word had an aspirated H on each end, but aspirated H's that showed no mercy: H W I T H H!

"Without pain!" blanched the husband.

Soon the nitrous oxides, the chloroforms, the chloromethanes, poured thick and fast upon the unhappy man's organism.

A few moments later, in the adjoining office, as the beautiful Madame Lecoq-Hue feebly protested:

"Come on, get up, if my husband..."

"Ah, your husband!" cried Surgeon with a burst of laughter. "Your husband... You can't imagine how well he's sleeping!"

And, as both of them had predicted, they weren't bored.

Irony

It's a tavern, decorated in the purest Louis-Philippe.

It would be hard to imagine a place more old-fashioned, or more lugubrious.

Yellowed marble tables stretch out, devoid of customers.

In the back, an old pool table takes on the look of a moldy catafalque, and the three balls (even the red) are the same yellow as the tables, with all the gaiety of forgotten bones.

In one corner, a small group of clients, apparently from the same era, play an interminable game of dominoes; their tiles and their fingers clatter like skeletons. Occasionally, the old men speak, and every sentence begins, "Back in our day..."

At the bar, behind bottles of outdated Vespetro and outmoded Parfait Amour, stands the hostess, glum and desiccated, with long curls of the same pale yellow as her tables and billiard balls.

The waiter, old and bald, who treats the hostess with familiarity (he must have worked there for years), prowls among the empty tables like a lost soul.

Then three young men enter, obviously lost.

They're received with open hostility by the domino

players and the waiter. Only the woman at the bar attempts a vague smile, perhaps retrospective.

She remembers that young men used to be a good thing, long ago.

The newcomers, somewhat startled at first by the chilly ambience, sit down. Suddenly, one of them approaches the bar.

"Madame," he says, with the most polished urbanity, "we might happen to die of laughter in your establishment. If such a tragedy does occur, please return our bodies to our respective families. Here's the address."

Tickets

A Memento from the 1889 Universal Exposition

"I buy tickets!"

I often stopped awhile by that woman, who lost her breath shouting and reshouting that desperate cry, and not once did I see her engage in the slightest transaction.

"I buy tickets!"

It's true that the purchaser's exterior aspect offered no illusion to ticket holders. Her shoes were certainly not soiled with mud from the Pactolus, and neither was the hem of her skirt.

Her voice, above all, precluded any idea of available capital, a voice hoarse from an ailment that I diagnosed as boozoid and vagabondiform crapulitis.

Imagine one of those dark and thin women, seemingly modeled with a few cuts of a saber, with nothing going for her but her eyes, but those going very well.

"I buy tickets!"

Me, I was quite fond of her, that tall gal, and if I had any tickets to sell, would gladly have given them for nothing, for her eyes.

Her eyes! Her eyes, in which all of the rest of her seemed to be concentrated!

Her eyes, where whole squadrons of hearts could have evolved at their leisure!

"I buy tickets!"

Now, toward the end of the Exposition, my uncle Alcide Toutaupoil turned up at my place.

"I decided at the last minute," he said, "to count on you to show me the beauties of the Exposition, without wasting my time."

My uncle Toutaupoil is a serious man, a solicitor in a little town in the north-east of the center of France, and which professional discretion prevents me from indicating more clearly.

A capable archeologist, my uncle enjoys an enviable reputation in all the local scholarly societies, and his memoir, *Potsherds Through the Ages* (with 14 intaglio plates), is found in all libraries worthy of the name.

This is enough to indicate that Alcide Toutaupoil showed no serious vocation for the role of gonfalonier in modern dissipation.

"Belly dancing? You want to show me belly dancing? Don't think of it, my poor friend! I didn't come to Paris for that!"

"But uncle, it's ethnography, after all. You can never really know a civilization, if you persist, under the pretext of modesty, in avoiding certain spectacles, which, certainly, offend our most intimate sentiments, but which nevertheless offer a fruitful education. Science has its demands, uncle!"

Thus it was that I convinced my austere relative to offer me various refreshments in the more amusing parts of the Exposition. I knew the Machine Gallery, and I had seen enough of the retrospective altarpieces.

"I buy tickets!"

One day, I showed him the tall woman, with those eyes that were even bigger, who offered to buy so many tickets and bought so few.

My uncle almost had a fit!

"What?" he cried. "You, whom I knew once as almost rational, you cast your eyes on such creatures! It's enough to make me think you have some genesic perversion!"

"Genesic" was harsh! I didn't insist.

"I buy tickets!"

Like everything under the sun, the Universal Exposition of 1889 came to a close, and I no longer saw my businesswoman with the eyes.

"I buy tickets!"

A few days later, I was strolling through the fair in Montmartre, when a booth caught my attention. It showed, according to the sign:

The beautiful Zim-laï-lah

The only true Exotic in the Fair

In the crowd, a young woman of the people, leaning on the arm of a burly worker, asked the latter:

"What country are they from, the Exotics?"

"The Exotics?... Next to Algeria, you know!... a little bit to the left."

The young woman of the people gave the vigorous geographer a long look, redolent with admiration.

I went in to see the Exotic.

Zim-laï-lah, prettier than Fatima, my word! and seemingly as intelligent, presided amid almahs of no importance.

Among them...

"I buy tickets!"

Among them, her, the tall dark woman with the eyes!

After the show, we chatted:

"Say, your friend, the old man you took to the Exposition..."

"Yes?"

"Well! He sure likes the ladies... For example, he was

pretty nice to me! We spent two hours together, and he gave me more than two hundred tickets!"

"I buy tickets!"

A Little "Turn Of The Century"

—Say, uncle...

—Yes, my friend?

—You know what?... If you were very nice?

—If I were very nice?

—Yes... Well, you'd put an article of mine in the *Chat Noir*.

—What do you mean "put an article of yours"?

—Well, get a story I did printed, of course!

—What, you're making literature, you?

—Why not?... And no dumber than your stuff, you know.

—How pretentious!

—Pretentious?... Pretentious to think I'm as clever as this guy!... Oh la la, aren't you hoity-toity, old man!

—!!!... And so, you want to make your debut in the press?

—Yes, I wrote a little story, I want to give it to you, and you'll get it printed. I won't put my name on it, because I'd never hear the end of it from mama. You sign it, but we'll split the take.

—You're starting early, being practical!

—Hey, if you're not practical at seven, when will you be?

—Where is this masterpiece?

—Here.

STORY OF A BAD LITTLE BARTENDER
AND A GOOD LITTLE LAMP SELLER

To the Misses Manitou and Tonton.

Once upon a time, on the boulevard de Courcelles, there was a lousy little jerk who was the son of a wine seller.

Nobody in the neighborhood liked him, because he was a dirty little kid who played jokes on everyone.

He had awful red hair that stuck out all over, big ears that stuck out from his head, and a little snub nose like those dogs that kill rats, and then red splotches all over his face.

He made so much noise with his whip, he sounded like a real coachman.

Next to his father's store, there was a man who sold lamps, and also buckets, watering cans, and zinc pitchers.

So the little bartender went over there to hammer on all the utensils to make noise and bother the neighbors.

The lamp seller had a little girl who was as nice as the little boy was disagreeable.

You can't imagine anything sweeter and more charming than that little girl.

She had blue eyes, a fine little nose, a pretty little mouth, and fine blonde hair, so fine that when there was just one, you couldn't even see it.

When it was nice out, she sat on her little folding chair on the sidewalk, and she learned her lessons, and when she knew her lessons, she just sat there.

At that moment, the little bartender came up behind her, and pulled her ponytail going "ding ding ding," like her ponytail was a bell rope on a steamship.

That really annoyed the little lamp seller. But one day she had an idea. She took some money from the cashbox and gave it to her papa's little apprentice, who was very strong, and who gave the little bartender a few good punches in the nose, and a few good kicks in the legs.

The little bartender told his parents that he fell on the ground, and that was why his nose was bleeding.

The next day, he went back to pull the poor little lamp seller's ponytail.

So, the little lamp seller gets mad and wonders what she

can do to play a good trick on the bad little bartender.

This is what she did:

She invited him to a tea party, one Thursday, with her and some other girls.

They began by eating cakes, grapes, and everything, and then she said:

"Now we'll drink some white wine."

And she filled their glasses with the gasoline they used for the lamps.

The little girls had been warned, so they didn't drink any, but the bad little bartender gulped it all down.

He was sick as a horse, and even his mama thought he was done for, but he was so stubborn that he wouldn't say what happened.

Fortunately, they had a good doctor who made him well.

When he was well, he went to kiss the little lamp seller, and said he was sorry for all his tricks, and after that, he never pulled her ponytail or hammered on the watering cans.

He became very nice, his hair turned less red, his red splotches went away, his ears pulled back, and his nose stopped looking like the muzzle of a butcher's dog.

And then, when he grew up, he married the little lamp seller and they had lots of children.

They sent all the boys to the Polytechnic School.

Signed: TOTO

—So, uncle, what do you think of my story?

—Very interesting, but your young lamp seller seems to be quite a nasty little creature.

—Absolutely!

—Well! And so?

—And so what? You didn't understand the whole story is ironic?... Huh! How about that! I didn't think you were so naive!

(*The sound of a kick in the behind rings out.*)

Inflame the Bacchante

The rich collector studied the picture for a long time.

It was a beautiful picture, freshly painted, which showed a nude bacchante, leaning back.

One could tell she was a bacchante by the bunch of grapes she was eating. And besides, she had vine branches in her hair, like all self-respecting bacchantes, or even those without self respect.

The rich collector was satisfied, but not truly satisfied.

Anxiously, the young painter awaited the rich collector's decision.

"My God, yes," the latter said, "it's very good... It's not bad at all, even... The head is pretty... So is the torso... It's well painted... Those grapes make my mouth water, but... Your bacchante doesn't seem... How can I put it?... Inflamed enough."

"You would have preferred a drunk woman, then!" the artist timidly replied.

"No, not drunk! But... How can I put it?... Inflamed."

The artist said nothing, but scratched his head.

For once, the rich collector was right. The bacchante was as pretty as possible, but rather rational, for a bacchante.

"So, my young friend," concluded the capitalist, "spend

a few more hours on it. I'll come back tomorrow morning. Meanwhile, try to... How did I put it?"

"Inflame the bacchante!"

"That's it."

And the capitalist disappeared.

"Inflame the bacchante," the young painter bravely repeated to himself. "Inflame the bacchante!"

The model who had posed for the picture was a splendid strapping eighteen year old, certainly the possessor of the most beautiful torso in Paris, and most of the suburbs.

I'm quite sure that if you knew this model, you'd never want another.

And the head was worthy of the torso, and the rest of the body worthy of the head and torso. So!...

But, unfortunately, a bit cold.

One day when she was posing for Gustave Boulanger, the master said to her, with a tinge of impatience:

"But inflame yourself a bit, for heaven's sake!... You'd think you were a government model."

(An inappropriate quip, just between us, coming from a member of the Institute.)

Our young artist hurried to his model.

The young lady was still asleep.

He made her get up, get dressed, all with professional discretion, and brought her back to his place.

He had an idea.

They had lunch together, at his place.

The spiciest foods covered the table, and the champagne flowed with the same overabundance as the waters of heaven.

And, after lunch, I hope you will believe that, for an inflamed bacchante, she was an inflamed bacchante.

And the young painter was also inflamed.

She resumed her pose.

"Good Lord!" he cried. "That's it!"

You can believe it was it.

She was leaning back a bit too much. Her cheeks glowed with a joyful carmine.

An infinitely delicate rosy pink tinted—oh so lightly!—the impeccable ivory of her queenly breasts.

Her eyes were almost closed, but between her long lashes, you glimpsed the laughing sparkle of her tipsy little eyes.

And in the incomparable purple of her half-open mouth, shone the humid and inviting nacre of her beautiful choppers.

The next day, when the rich collector returned, he found the studio locked.

He went up to the apartment and knocked with countless *toc tocs*.

"My bacchante!" he shouted, "My bacchante!"

Finally, a voice wafted from the back of the alcove, the

voice of the bacchante herself, and the voice replied:

"Not done yet."

Fancy Dress

After a spree even more exorbitant than its predecessors —and God knows there were many of impressive caliber among its predecessors!—the young viscount Guy de La Hurlotte was invited by his father to serve a five year engagement in the French infantry.

Guy, whose motto was that one could have fun anywhere, asked only that he be sent not too far from Paris.

"Why not right to the barracks in the Pépinière, two steps from the boulevard?" roared the terrible count. "No, my boy, you're going to Senegal."

The countess broke down sobbing. Senegal! Does anyone come back from Senegal!

"To Algeria, then."

Finally, after fresh maternal outcries, they agreed on L..., a small camp in Normandy, rather gloomy and totally devoid of nocturnal restaurants.

Guy's entry into military existence exactly matched its remarkable civilian antecedents.

With that charming carelessness and aristocratic ease that were the envy of all his friends, Guy, armed with his instructions, found the officer in charge of the regiment's records, known as the *great major*.

"Good morning, ladies and gentlemen... Oh, sorry! There are no ladies, and I regret it... The great major, please?"

"It is I," said a tall bony man in a jacket, with a peevish expression.

"What? You're the great major?" Guy replied, overcome with astonishment. "You had to tell me yourself or I wouldn't have believed it... You don't look great at all... And you don't seem too major, either! When they told me about the great major, the word evoked in my mind a kind of decorated barrel. I get here, and what do I find?... Some sort of civilian beanpole."

The officer, already thoroughly offended by these impertinent remarks, leapt to his feet with rage and indignation when he learned they were offered by a simple recruit, a "rookie"!

The young viscount's attitude received an immediate compensation in the form of eight days confinement to barracks.

"And besides," added the officer, "I'll be sure to indicate you to your captain."

"I hope you will, my great major, and I thank you in advance. One can never be indicated enough to one's superiors."

Such beginnings were promising; they did not disappoint.

Guy de La Hurlotte immediately became the favorite of the regiment, where he brought, to the accomplishment of his military duties, so much imagination and such a penchant for the unexpected, that discipline did not always receive its due.

But could one hold it against him, that devilish viscount, so charming, such a good boy, always with his heart on his sleeve and a Havana in his hand?

With the small sums he received from his parents, and the extensive credit he procured in town, Guy led the lavish life of a grand lord, who paid little attention to edicts and rules.

However, during the first days of his enlistment, the young viscount was "hit with," as they say in the army, two days in the guardhouse.

Passing with his company through the main street in L..., Guy had directed a passionate declaration and countless kisses to a young woman who, from her balcony, was watching the troops.

Enraged at this poor conduct, Captain Lemballeur, as soon as they returned, sentenced him with the following words:

Showed within the ranks a tempestuous and gesticulatory comportment inappropriate to a soldier of the second class.

As you might think, Guy had a field day with this phrase. The words "tumultuous" and "gesticulatory" became popular both in the regiment and in town, and poor Captain Lemballeur never dared punish Guy again.

The Colonel himself seemed powerless against his good humored attitude, and whenever one of the viscount's jokes reached his ears, he simply shrugged his shoulders, and murmured, "Oh, that La Hurlotte!"

I won't try to describe in detail all the military adventures of our joyous friend. The largest paper available would not suffice.

I'll content myself, if you like, with recounting the episode that, for me, marked the culmination of his imaginative career.

It was Sunday. Guy was on guard duty.

At ten o'clock in the evening, he assumed his post at the magazine, some two or three hundred meters from headquarters.

That evening, there was great excitement around the magazine. Some people nearby were giving a big costume ball for all the brilliant society of L...

A few guests (Guy was as familiar in town as he was popular in the regiment) recognized, in the humble sentry, the brilliant viscount. There was one common cry:

"Well! La Hurlotte, will you join us this evening?"

"I'm terribly sorry, but it's very difficult for me to get away at the moment. I've been entrusted with the protection of this edifice, and if it were stolen in my absence, I'd be forced to reimburse the government, which would only upset my poor papa, already so overwhelmed."

"Can't you get a substitute?"

"Say, there's an idea."

It was an idea, in fact, a bad idea, of course; but for Guy, a bad idea was always better than no idea at all.

At that very moment, a soldier walked by, a little timid blond one.

"Would you like to earn a hundred sous, Baudru?"

"I wouldn't turn it down... but doing what?"

"Taking over my guard duty, until a quarter of midnight."

Baudru immediately trembled before this incorrect proposition, but damn! a hundred sous...

"Okay," he decided, "give me your pack and your rifle, and above all, don't be late."

Guy's entrance was a sensation.

He had found in the vestibule a superb suit of armor into which he had inserted himself, and arrived, helmet on head, lance in fist, swaggering like in the old tournaments.

His opponents were represented by several plates of petit fours and cups of tea, which soon crashed to the floor.

The lady of the house began to show serious concern for the rest of her porcelain, when Baudru, pale as death, rushed into the salon.

"Hurry up and come downstairs, La Hurlotte! There's a bunch of officers coming. Here, take your rifle and pack."

A whole world of terror wheeled through Guy's brain. The articles of the Military Code flamed before his eyes, in livid characters: Court-martial... Abandonment of post... Death!

All that in three seconds!... Then his composure abruptly returned.

To get rid of the armor was out of the question. The officers would have ten times enough time to get there.

"My God, too bad! I'll have to go down like this. I'll explain it somehow."

He was just in time. The officer and an orderly with a torch were no more than fifty meters from the sentry box. Bravely, Guy assumed his position, grasped his lance, and, in a loud voice, somewhat muffled by the lowered visor, cried, "Halt!... Who goes there?"

At this sudden apparition, the soldier dropped his torch, and the brave Captain Lemballeur, for it was he, could not suppress his strong emotions.

If La Hurlotte's ancestors had returned to earth at that moment, they would have been satisfied with their descendant, for Guy, clad in steel, helmet on head, lance in position, looked truly dashing.

Moonlight illuminated the scene.

However, the Captain's surprise soon came to an end.

"I assume it's you again, La Hurlotte?"

After many attempts, Guy finally managed to raise the visor of his helmet.

"I can explain, Captain... Since it's rather cold tonight..."

"Yes, my boy, still at it. I'm all too aware that you have no shortage of nerve, but this is decidedly too much! Do me the pleasure of returning that tinplate where you found it... and then you'll hear from me."

Guy finished his duty filled with keen anxiety, an unaccustomed emotion for him.

As for Captain Lemballeur, he was no less anxious about how to word his description of La Hurlotte's punishment, for his colleagues still ridiculed him for his famous "tempestuous and gesticulatory comportment."

He returned to headquarters, asked for the book, scratched his head for awhile, and wrote:

Two days in the guardhouse for Pvt. La Hurlotte. While on guard duty, he wore fancy dress.

Aphasia

That, for example, surpassed all the fishy stories Captain Lemballeur had ever heard, and, hellfire and damnation! he'd heard some fishy ones, had Captain Lemballeur, in all of his campaigns, in the Crimea, in Mexico, and everywhere, and everywhere, hellfire and damnation!

The doctor, a young major fresh from Val-de-Grâce, was unresponsive.

"But really," the Captain thundered, "you don't expect me to believe that this hellfire and damnation bugler is not mocking me outright!"

"I don't think so myself, Captain, because in the hospital I've seen cases of aphasia even stranger than this."

"Aphasia... Aphasia! I don't give a damn for your aphasia, myself... with eight days in the guardhouse!"

"As a physician, it's my responsibility to forbid any injury to this man, whom I provisionally consider a patient, and a very interesting patient, at that. I'm sending him to the hospital today for observation."

The excellent Captain Lemballeur bowed before the man of science; but, even so, hellfire and damnation! It sounded fishy to him!

During this colloquy, there were, in one of the rooms

on the third floor of the fourth building, two men who had never laughed so much.

When I say two men, I should say one viscount and one bugler.

The viscount was a private second class, of elegant appearance, responding to the name of Guy de La Hurlotte.

Following several sprees surpassing the usual proportions of acceptable sprees, the old Count de La Hurlotte had invited his son to serve a five year engagement in the French infantry, and that was how Guy became the pride and joy of the 145th line in L...

The bugler then sharing the viscount's expansive mood was none other than his batman and faithful friend, Jumet by name.

And they had twice as much to laugh about, the scamps!

First, because the previous day's adventure had been thoroughly amusing in itself, and then because, having threatened to turn out badly, it finished better than they could have dreamed.

The day before, Sunday, Guy was confined to the barracks, as happened to him more often than was his share.

It was a beautiful day. On the stroke of four, Guy could no longer resist; he put on his finest clothes and left the barracks.

As it happened, it was the bugler Jumet, the devoted Jumet, who was on guard.

"Say, Jumet," Guy remarked, "I'm confined to barracks, but I'm going out anyway."

"Be careful not to get caught, you old viscount."

"No danger of that; I'm off to have dinner with an adulterous wife."

"Have fun."

"If the master sergeant summons the recruits, don't sound the call, okay?"

"Damn! That's pretty inconvenient."

"Just play something else, that's all."

And Jumet, who, like his friend Guy, never worried about anything, simply replied:

"Understood, viscount; bring me back a good cigar."

"I'll bring you two, but I don't like putting conditions on favors."

And, with a cordial handshake, the viscount and the bugler separated.

Unfortunately for the viscount, he had not stepped a hundred meters from the barracks, when he saw the terrible Captain Lemballeur, the very man who had confined him there.

With admirable agility, Guy ducked into the first shop that came to hand, but not quickly enough for the Captain not to recognize him.

Delighted at catching La Hurlotte in the act, Captain Lemballeur returned to the barracks with giant strides.

"Bugler!" he cried. "Assemble the recruits, hellfire and damnation! And hop to it!"

Poor Jumet, that was just his luck!

He tried to negotiate.

"Captain, the master sergeant has just ordered Recall."

"I don't give a damn! Assemble them again, hellfire and damnation!"

Slowly, sadly, reluctantly, Jumet seized his instrument and walked to the middle of the courtyard.

Tarata... Ta! Tarata... Ta! Tarata... Ta!

"You idiot!" cried Lemballeur. "I told you to assemble the recruits, hellfire and damnation! Not the corporals!"

"Ah, sorry, Captain. I beg your pardon."

Tarata... tatata! Tarata... tatata!

"Now he's assembling the sergeants! Hellfire and damnation, he's as drunk as a pig!"

Jumet apologized again, and successively sounded Mess Call, Pay Call, Sick Call, Mail Call, Reveille, etc... But not Assembly.

The whole barracks was thrown upside down.

Captain Lemballeur consisted of one great explosion of "Hellfire and damnation!"

He seized Jumet by the collar:

"Hellfire and damnation! Will you sound Assembly, yes

or no?"

Jumet gently extricated himself, and in a resolute yet desolate tone:

"I'm very sorry, Captain," he said, "but I CAN'T REMEMBER THE TUNE."

And he returned to the barracks, in all simplicity.

The most terrible threats, readings from the Code of Military Justice, nothing worked.

"When you shoot me," he answered with utter resignation, "what do you expect from me? I can't remember the tune."

The next morning, on Guy de La Hurlotte's advice, Jumet reported to the infirmary, and explained his case to the doctor.

"What happened to me yesterday was very strange. Captain Lemballeur ordered me to sound Assembly, and I couldn't remember the tune for the life of me. Something in my head must be broken."

The doctor interrogated him on his medical and family history.

"I have a sister who's a little screwy," Jumet replied, "and an uncle who's completely nuts."

"Obviously, this is a very curious case of aphasia."

Jumet was subjected to visits from all the bigwigs in military medicine, who unanimously recognized aphasia, with the beginnings of paralysis.

And the bugler Jumet was discharged at the first general inspection.

With this adventure, Guy de La Hurlotte lost the cream of batmen and the pearl of friends, but civilian society gained, *raram avem*, a citizen who keeps his word.

A Bizarre Death

The highest tide of the century (it's the fifteenth I've seen, and I fervently hope that the series doesn't end any time soon) occurred last Tuesday, November 6th.

A delightful spectacle, which I wouldn't have traded for a cannonball, or even two cannonballs, or three.

Favored by a strong wind from the southwest, the lapping sea rose level with the quays of le Havre, and flooded the sewers of the town, mixing with the waste water, which it then discharged into the citizens' cellars.

The doctors rubbed their hands: "Good!" they said to themselves. "More typhoid for us!"

For, if you can believe it, le Havre-de-Grâce is built so that the sewers are above sea level. Thus, at the smallest tide, despite M. Rispal's energetic resistance, the le Havrians' offal overflows, cynically, onto the city's poshest arteries.

Doesn't it seem, parenthetically, that that filthy swine[1] François I, instead of leading an indolent existence in the brasseries of Carrefour de Buci, should have paid more attention to his kingdom's roads and bridges?

No matter! It was a beautiful sight.

I spent most of the day on the jetty, watching boats come in and others go out.

Since the wind was turning cooler, I turned up the collar on my overcoat. I was about to do the same with my trouser cuffs (I'm very particular about my appearance), when my friend Axelsen appeared.

My friend Axelsen is a young Norwegian painter, full of talent and sentimentality.

He has talent when he's hungry, and sentimentality the rest of the time.

At that moment, his sentimentality prevailed.

Was it the brisk wind? Was it his overflowing heart?... His eyes filled with tears.

"Well!" I said cordially. "Is something wrong, Axelsen?"

"I'm all right. A superb spectacle, but a painful memory. All of the 'highest tides of the century' break my poor heart."

"Tell me about it."

"Gladly, but not here."

And he took me to a little place behind a tobacconist's, where a young English woman, rather pretty, served us a very special *svensk punsch*.

Axelsen dried his tears, and this is the harrowing tale that he told me:

"It was five years ago. I lived in Bergen (Norway), and was just starting in the arts. One day, one evening rather, at a ball given by M. Isdahl, the wealthy roe dealer, I fell in love with a charming young woman, who, at first sight, was not completely indifferent toward me. I met her father, and became friendly with the household. Her birthday was coming up. I wanted to give her a present, but what present?... Do you know Vågen Bay?"

"Not yet."

"Well, it's a very lovely bay, which my friend adored, especially one little part of it. I said to myself: 'I'll paint a pretty watercolor of this little part for her, she'll like that.' And one fine morning, off I go with my watercolor supplies. I forgot only one thing, my friend: water. Now you know that although dilution is illegal for wine sellers, it's practically indispensable for watercolorists. No water! My word, I said to myself, I'll just mix my watercolors with seawater, I'll see if that works.

"It made for a very pretty watercolor, which I gave to my friend, and which she promptly hung in her room. Except... Do you know what happened?"

"I will when you tell me."

"Well, it happened that the sea in my watercolor, painted with seawater, was sensitive to lunar attraction, and subject to tides. Nothing was more bizarre, my friend, than to see, in my painting, that little sea come in, in, in, covering the rocks, then go out, out, out, leaving them bare, gradually."

"Ah!"

"Yes... One night there was, like today, the highest tide of the century, and there was a terrifying storm on the coast. Tempest, thunder, hurricane!

"The next morning, I went to the villa where my lover lived. I found everyone in wild despair.

"My watercolor had overflown: the young lady was drowned in her bed."

"My poor friend!"

Axelsen wept like a seal. I squeezed his hand.

"And you know," he added, "everything I told you is absolutely true. Ask Johanson."

That very evening, I saw Johanson, who told me it was all a joke.

---

1. If, by chance, one of the monarch's descendants is offended by my characterization, he can come find me. I have never backed down from a Valois.

Mockery Punished[1]

I wanted to tell this story, on the occasion of the upcoming year, to demonstrate to young people disposed to mockery that it's always unseemly, and sometimes dangerous, to ridicule the unfortunate. I pray to heaven that this tale produce its desired effect, and that the new year be free of deplorable jokes and cruel taunts!

It was December 31, 1826.

It had snowed for several days on the little town of Potinbourg-sur-Bec, but the thaw had come, and the snow was turning into black mud.

At the corner of rue Saint-Gaspard and the place du Marché-aux-Veaux, stood the shop of Hume-Mabrize, master apothecary, for, back then, pharmacists were still unknown.

They sold drugs, not medicine. And, just between us, our poor world was none the worse for it.

It must have been around five o'clock in the evening.

Hume-Mabrize, in his laboratory, was elaborating who knows what electuary. The shop was under the care of the young Athanase, a budding apothecary of great promise, but, unfortunately, endowed with a caustic and mocking attitude.

At that time, having no work to do, Athanase stood in the doorway, watching people wading through the mud, and taking great pleasure in this cruel contemplation.

A large poultry and egg cart drove down rue Saint-Gaspard, at top speed, splattering the pedestrians, who shouted and shook their fists at that brute of a driver.

Right in front of the apothecary's shop, there was a wide and deep expanse of mud.

A man, a stranger to the area, had just enough time, to avoid being run over, to jump onto the sidewalk. But the wheels of the cart violently struck the puddle, and splashed its contents in every direction.

The stranger was literally inundated with muck. He got it in his shorts, all over his overcoat, on his face, even in his hair.

Athanase expressed unbridled joy at the accident. He burst out laughing, and, as the man walked away grumbling, called him back, to ask sarcastically:

"Would you like a brush?"

The next day was the first of the year.

Hume-Mabrize's shop had just opened, when a boy from the Roi-Maure Hotel came to request an emollient enema for a guest who was doubled over with severe abdominal pain.

All right," the apothecary replied. "As soon as he's ready, Athanase will go administer it himself."

At that time, as you know, the great Dr. Éguisier had not yet invented his ingenious device, and enemas were almost always administered by apothecaries themselves, or their assistants.

How a single invention can change our customs!

Hume-Mabrize prepared, with his usual care, a fine emollient liquid, sedative and mucilaginous, poured it still boiling into that tin cylinder you know so well, and there's my Athanase off to accomplish his mission.

The traveler's key was in the door. Athanase entered.

Without a word, the traveler uncovered the relevant part.

Athanase, with professional care and precision, did his duty.

Gently, without hurrying, the piston plunged into the cylinder, pushing before it the beneficial liquid, like a docile herd of sheep, soft and warm.

There... done!

There was nothing left but to withdraw it and to leave.

But suddenly, like a volcano, like an explosion, an unexpected phenomenon occurred.

Violently ejected, the healing liquid exited, as if disgraced at being brought to such a place.

Athanase's face was right there, in point-blank range. He didn't miss a drop.

The traveler then turned his other face toward the

young apothecary, and asked in a tone of polite courtesy:

"Would you like a brush?"

---

1. This little story was published five years ago, an important detail that will prevent any confusion with a similar story—*oh, how similar!*—that recently appeared over the signature of a pale young man whose father accused me, before Yvette Guilbert, of owing him two months' rent, which is untrue.

Oddities

We are told that the sultan Mahmoud by
his perpetual wars...

SIR CORDON SONNETT

By a bizarre example of the association of ideas (fairly common in the young men of my generation), the Exposition of 1889 reminded me of the one in 1878.

At that time, ten springs fewer bedecked my brow. It's terrifying how much one can age between two Universal Expositions, especially when they're separated by a considerable time.

My girlfriend then, a little brunette for whom the most cunning ecclesiastic would have given communion without confession (whereas a night of orgy, to her, was just a game), said to me one morning at breakfast:

"What are you going to do for the Exposition?"

"What should I do for the Exposition?"

"Exhibit."

"Exhibit?... What?"

"Anything."

"But I haven't invented anything!"

(At that time, I had not yet invented my aquarium with

frosted glass, for timid fish. Patent pending.)

"So," she continued, "buy a booth and show some freak."

"What freak?... You?"

Enraged, she replied with a frown:

"A freak, me?"

And she might have given me a few good slaps, when I cried, in a tone of amorous reconciliation:

"Yes, you're a freak, dear soul! Freakishly graceful, charming and fresh!"

Which was no lie, because she really was awfully nice, the little slut.

A coquettish nose, a mouth that was a bit large (but so well furnished), abundant silky hair, and that kind of tenderly pink-white skin that only women who use cream possess.

Of course, I wouldn't have thrown myself into the fountain in the place Pigalle for her, but I was fond of her just the same.

To make peace, I concluded:

"Good! Because it would please you, I'll show a freak."

"And me, I'll collect the money?"

"You can collect the money."

"And if I make mistakes when I make change, you won't beat me?"

"Have I ever beaten you?"

"I never made change, so I don't know..."

If I report this dialogue in detail, it's to give my clientele an idea of the conversations I had with Eugénie (or maybe her name was Bertha).

A week later, I received from London a midget, a pretty little midget.

When English midgets, as everyone knows, decide to be small, they defy the most powerful microscopes; but when they decide to be nasty, as is less known, they do so to the point of temerity.

That was the case with mine. Oh, the little nuisance!

He took an instant dislike to me, and his sole preoccupation was to cause me a constant string of keen disappointments and afflictions of all kinds.

When it came time for him to be exhibited, he stood on tiptoe with such skill that he looked as tall as you or I.

Then, when my friends mocked me, saying, "He's none too impressive, that midget of yours!", and I reported those insulting remarks to him, he cynically replied, in English:

"What do you expect?... Everyone has his off days."

One evening, I returned home two hours earlier than my business that day would seem to indicate.

Guess who I found, sharing Clara's bed (I remember now, her name was Clara)?

No sense trying, you'll never guess.

My midget! Yes, ladies and gentlemen, Clara was cheating on me with that minuscule Britisher!

I flew into such a rage!...

Fortunately for the traitor, I raised my arms to the heavens before punching him. He made use of the time it took me to lower them to his height to escape.

I never saw him again.

As for Clara, she literally doubled over with laughter under the covers.

"It's no laughing matter," I said severely.

"What do you mean, no laughing matter? What's wrong with you, anyway?... You big idiot, you're not jealous of an English midget? It was just to see, that's all. You have no idea..."

And she started laughing even harder, after which she told me a few details, truly comical, that succeeded in placating me.

Nevertheless, after that I remained suspicious of midgets, and, to use the space I'd rented, procured myself a Japanese giant.

Do you remember the Japanese giant of 1878? Well, I was the one who showed him. My Japanese giant bore no resemblance to my English midget.

Considerably taller, he was also good, obliging, and chaste.

Or, at least, he seemed to possess those qualities. I have reason to say "seemed to," because, after a few days, I made a discovery that floored me.

One evening, returning unexpectedly to Camille's room (yes, it was Camille, I remember now), I found, strewn across the floor, my giant's Oriental cast-offs, and in the bed, Camille with... guess with whom!

No sense trying, you'll never guess.

Camille, with my former midget!

It was that little swine of an English midget, who found that the best way to stay close to Camille was to disguise himself as a Japanese giant.

This escapade disgusted me forever with the life of a showman.

It was around this time that, entirely ruined by my mistress's extravagances, I took a position as valet, at 59, rue de Douai, with a certain Sarcey.

The Calf

A Christmas Story for Sara Salis

—Once upon a time, there was a little boy who was very good, very good. So for Christmas, his papa got him a calf.

—A real one?

—Yes, Sara, a real one.

—With flesh and skin?

—Yes, Sara, with flesh and skin.

—Who walked on his feet?

—I told you, a real calf!

—Then what?

—Then, the little boy was quite pleased to have a little calf. However, because he did dirty things on the living room floor...

—The little boy?

—No, the calf... Because he did dirty things, and made noise, and broke his little sisters' toys...

—The calf had little sisters?

—No, the little boy's little sisters... So he built a shed in the garden, a pretty little wooden shed...

—With little windows?

—Yes, Sara, with lots of little windows, and glass of many colors... That night, it was New Year's Eve. The little boy's papa and mama were invited to a lady's house for dinner. So, after the little boy had his supper, he went to bed and his parents left...

—They left him all alone in the house?

—No, the maid was there... Except the little boy didn't go to sleep. He was just pretending. When the maid went to bed, the little boy got up and went looking for his little friends who lived next door...

—He went outside naked?

—Oh no, he got dressed. So all of these nasty little boys, who wanted to celebrate New Year's Eve like the grown-ups, came into the house. But they were out of luck, because the kitchen and dining room were locked. So what did they do?

—Tell me, what did they do?

—They went down into the garden and ate the calf.

—Raw?

—Raw, completely raw.

—Oh, what bad boys!

—Since raw veal is very hard to digest, all of those nasty little brats were very sick the next day. It's a good thing the doctor came! He gave them lots of herbal tea to drink, and they got better... But ever since then, they never gave the little boy any veal.

—And what did the little boy say?

—The little boy? Oh, he didn't give a damn.

Traveling

SIMPLE NOTES

Unlike many people I could name, I prefer to find a seat in a train compartment that is almost full, rather than practically empty.

For many reasons.

First, it irritates people.

Are you like me? I love to irritate people, because people are all filthy swine who disgust me.

There's some filthy swine for you, those people!

And besides, I love to hear stupid things said around me, and God knows people are stupid! Have you noticed?

Finally, I prefer a full compartment to an empty compartment because the lack of comfort lacerates my flesh, hardens my heart, armors my soul, and prepares me for the harsh struggles of life.

Which is why, no later than the day before yesterday, I boarded a car in which all the seats were taken, except one, which I seized, not without joy.

A second reason (perhaps the better one) compelled me to enter that compartment rather than another, and that was because the others were just as crowded.

This event, to which I attach perhaps undue importance,

occurred in a small station whose name you will permit me to omit, since it connects to a region well-stocked with game and still largely unexplored.

Among the travelers in my car I will mention:

Two young lovers, fervently hoping for tunnels, hand in hand, eye to eye. An idyll!

It recalls my tender youth. A tear plashes[1] from my eye, and, after trembling awhile on my lashes, runs down my hollow cheeks to lose itself in the bristles of my rough mustache.

Continue, young lovers, to love one another, and you, young man, put your hand for awhile in your mistress's hand, that's better than putting it in her face, especially violently.

Next to the lovers, there was a fat and undistinguished ecclesiastic, upon whose soutane one could see the remains of ancient sauces deposited there from negligence while eating.

If I were you, mister priest, I'd divert a few funds from Peter's Pence to buy myself some napkins.

Next to the ecclesiastic, a very nice young painter, whom I've since befriended.

Very talented and highly amusing.

Next to the door, a man and his son.

The man is pushing forty, the little boy has just seen effloresce, this year, his sixth spring. Poor little guy!

The father profits from the hours of travel to inculcate some grammar into his offspring. They're studying *Plurals*, those terrible *Plurals*.

The words ending in *ouse* too, except for *house* and a few others whose memory has vanished from my brain.

When the unlucky little toad has squirreled the rule and exceptions away into his poor little noggin, the teacher goes on to the *examples*, and this is where he appears in all his beauty.

The child holds a blackboard on his knees and a chalk in his hand.

"Put this into the plural for me."

"Yes, papa."

"Pay attention."

"Yes, papa."

"*The louse and the mouse gave the souse a blouse.*"

At that moment, the young painter looks at me, I look at the young painter, and despite my celebrated composure, I burst out laughing, as does he.

The father-teacher, in full instructional mode, doesn't understand the reason for our hilarity, and continues:

"Now, here are some words with a double o, some of which take a double e, others a final s."

I await the example. It's not long in coming:

"*The goose and the moose found a tooth in a booth.*"

The little one makes a judicious distribution of e's and

s's, and we move on to geography.

No, you have no idea of the enormous quantity of rivers that throw themselves into the Mediterranean!

It seems that, in my day, there weren't as many as that.

My friend the artist gravely asks me why, on receiving all that water, the Mediterranean doesn't overflow.

I give him the classic reply: because Providence foresaw this catastrophe, and put sponges in the sea.

The little boy, who heard us, asks his father "if it's true."

The father, blindsided, imperceptibly shrugs his shoulders, doesn't answer, and declares the lesson over.

Encouraged by this result, we try to inculcate some false principles into the young lad.

"Do you know, my little friend, why the sea, although fed by freshwater rivers, is salty?"

"No, sir."

"Well, because there are salt-cod in it."

"Ah!"

"And that slate you have on your lap, do you know where it comes from?"

"No, sir."

"Well, it comes from the town of Angers, and that's why roofers are always angry."

At that moment, the man intervenes, and asks us not to give his son false information.

We reply with some asperity:

"And you claim you didn't fill him with misinformation first, when you made him write that *'geese and mooses find teeth in booths'*!" If you think Buffon would have liked to hear such heresies!"

We pulled into the station.

It was about time!

---

1. It is unfortunate that this expression is becoming outmoded, for it is significative and useful. Amyot used it in his translation of *Daphnis and Chloe*: "There was in that area a cavern called the cavern of the Nymphs, which was a large and heavy rock, at the end of which PLASHED a fountain which made a stream from which was irrigated the beautiful verdant meadow."

The Tumultoscope

I don't remember now, but I think it was the young Duke Honneau de la Lunerie who cried:

"No, man is not an animal; or if he's an animal, he's an animal who is superior."

At this last word, Laflemme lost his patience:

"A superior animal, man!... Would you like to hear my opinion of man?"

"Certainly, Laflemme."

"Man is an idiot, the worst idiot in creation."

"And woman?"

"Woman is the second worst."

"You're hard on humanity, Laflemme!"

"Not hard enough! It's precisely man's humanity that ruined him. To think that the idiot could have been the happiest of animals, if he could only keep quiet. But no, it wasn't enough for him to face rain from the skies, God's thunder, and disease, so he invented civilization."

"But, Laflemme," interrupted the young Duke Honneau de la Lunerie.

"There is no 'but,' Duke Honneau!" vehemented Laflemme. "Civilization, what is it, but the barracks, the office, the factory, the aperitif, and bank tellers?

"Man is so little the king of nature, that he's the only animal who can't do a thing without paying for it. The other animals eat on the house, drink on the house... love on the house..."

"May I remind you, Laflemme, that there are many humans who have no trouble practicing this last operation as architecturally as possible. There are some individuals who even make a small profit."

"Exactly! But with what opprobrium does humanity shower these ingenious and charming beings! I return to the question. Have you ever seen a stag ruin himself for a doe? Cannot the most debauched pig indulge all his swinishness without his colleagues, disguised as police sergeants or bailiffs, handing him an arrest warrant or promissory note?... Tell me frankly, can any of you boast of witnessing the spectacle of a possum pulling coins from its pouch?"

None of us accepted the challenge.

Laflemme was decidedly correct: *man is an inferior animal.*

The young Duke Hanneau de la Lunerie himself seemed crushed by the documentary eloquence of our fine friend Laflemme.

Our fine friend Laflemme was not, as one might assume, a paradoxical fantasist, an empty theoretician.

As soon as he left childhood, and even a bit before, he

had put into practice his theories on the contemptibility of work.

His favorite motto was: *We are not cattle.* His program: *Eat, drink, and be idle.*

The public demonstrations by those wild revolutionaries who demanded eight hours of work a day provoked him to gentle smiles, and he thanked with all his heart the guardians of the peace [*sic*] who clubbed those formidable idiots.

Laflemme possessed no personal fortune, nor any other. Employed nowhere, he would have been unwelcome trying to collect a salary.

The instinctive horror he had for the judicial system, and Mazas Prison in particular, kept him on the path of relative virtue.

He often happened to borrow sums that he neglected to return, but always from wealthy people who wouldn't be bothered by such transactions (a certain innate sensitivity took the place of his conscience).

Now and then, he performed pathetically remunerated tasks, but which took little effort, such as, for example, writing novels for M. Richebourg.

One that he wrote, under those conditions, has remained engraved upon the emptiest hearts of all true concierges. It was called, if I remember correctly:

The Beautiful Double Amputee,
or, The Daughter of the Stillborn Lunatic.

All of the money he obtained from this sensational work went, besides, to the upkeep of a charming young woman from Clignancourt, whom he kept as a mistress, and whose minuscule waist had earned her the nickname of Baby Zero-Point-Five.

Despite her small dimensions, Baby Zero-Point-Five was endowed with Cleopatrian appetites, and poor Laflemme had to hand her over, one fine evening, for ten sous, to a dead drunk Russian.

Winter was coming. Laflemme, naturally sensitive to the cold, and disgusted with wading through the icy mud of Paris, when it was so nice and sunny down south, decided to spend the winter in Nice.

He packed his trunks, which consisted of one elderly suitcase, removed the little hand from an old nickel watch he had, set the big hand at six, and took the train for Nice.

Still few people in Nice: the season was just starting.

Laflemme installed himself in a comfortable hotel, and, from his first dinner in the restaurant, keenly impressed the other guests.

The conversation turned, as it does in all hotel restaurants in Nice, every day that God makes, to the famous earthquake of 1886.

(In Nice, only four topics of conversation are permitted: the roulette at Monte Carlo, the earthquake of '86, any distinguished people who are arriving or leaving, and the generous pleasure one feels at staying warm while Parisians are shivering.)

"The earthquake!" said Laflemme in a quiet, but well articulated, voice. "From now on, if people are victims, it's only because they want to be."

Ears were cocked with interrogatory expressions.

"Exactly, because science now permits us to predict a catastrophe twenty-four hours before it happens."

With that, all the diners were hanging on Laflemme's every word.

"What? You never heard of the *tumultoscope*, that instrument invented by an Irish priest?"

None of the ladies and gentlemen had heard of the *tumultoscope*.

Laflemme produced his famous nickel watch.

"You see, it's not very complicated. The instrument somewhat resembles a watch, but has only one hand. Inside is an apparatus which is extremely sensitive to the earth's telluric currents. It's very easy to use. You place the instrument flat, like this, so that the hand is on the axis of the meridian, like that. If the hand stays on the number six, there's nothing to fear. If the hand moves to the right of the six, that means there are positive telluric currents. If, on the contrary, it points to the left, that indicates negative telluric currents, more dangerous than the others."

All eyes were fixed attentively on the hand of the watch, which stayed impassively on the number six.

"We can sleep soundly tonight," Laflemme cheerfully concluded.

From that day on, Laflemme was the spoiled child of the hotel. At lunch, at dinner, he had to bring out his tumultoscope.

"Nothing again today! Everything's fine!"

And the faces reflected serenity.

The morning of the seventh day, Laflemme came downstairs earlier than usual. He sought out the proprietor of the hotel.

"Be so good as to prepare my bill. I'll telegraph to Paris for money, and I'll leave this evening."

"Is anything wrong?"

"Take a look."

The tumultoscope read nine and a half. Negative telluric currents, the worst of all! It wouldn't be long.

The patron blanched.

"Above all, don't tell anybody. Your instrument might be wrong."

"Duty demands that I warn everyone."

"Don't do anything, I beg of you."

And the poor man kept getting paler. This revelation meant the hotel empty in an hour, the season lost, ruination!

"Here, M. Laflemme, your bill's taken care of, do me the courtesy of leaving at once."

"But I have no money for the trip."

"Here's 200 francs, but please leave without saying anything."

Laflemme gravely put the canceled bill in his wallet, the five louis in his change purse, and took the train.

He spent a delightful day in Cannes, and returned, the same evening, to check into an excellent hotel in Nice—not the same one, of course.

The tumultoscope aroused the same interest in the new location as in the preceding one.

I won't bore the reader with a monotonous recital of Laflemme's adventures in the hotels of Nice.

Suffice it to say that the business with the tumultoscope never failed.

The roulette at Monte Carlo, touched by such ingenuity, changed into an *alma parens* for Laflemme, who returned in the spring, healthy, fat, smiling, and not devoid of funds.

It was at that time that he added to his favorite, somewhat trivial motto, *We are not cattle*, the more elegant and neo-Darwinian *Scam for life!*

An Invention

Monologue for Cadet

If anyone had ever told me that I'd invent something, I would have been very surprised! And you know... not one of those minor inventions, those little nothings... No, a serious invention.

I can't say that it's one of those inventions that galvanize the century, no, but...!

It's funny how an invention comes to you... just when you least expect it.

It's the story of Christopher Columbus and the egg!

Discovering America was the furthest thing from Columbus's mind. And then his eyes fell upon a hard-boiled egg... He said to himself: ...I don't remember what he said, but at any rate it gave him the idea to discover America.

My invention didn't happen like that.

There's no hard-boiled egg with mine.

Me, I don't claim to be anything that I'm not. I don't have a mind like lightning, but I do have a certain logic, an inexorable logic, one of those logics that is... inexorable!

Here's how I found my invention.

It was raining heavily, one of those downpours! Oh,

what fine weather it was!

Next to rain like that, the universal flood would seem like a drought.

I had a number of errands to do. I found myself under the arches of the rue de Rivoli.

And I said to myself: What a pity that all of the streets in Paris aren't like the rue de Rivoli.

You would always be dry, under the arches, wherever you went. It would be charming!... If I were the government, I'd force the proprietors to build all of their houses with arches.

But perhaps that wouldn't be too liberal.

No, no arches, but what prevents shopkeepers from setting up canvas in front of their shops to shelter passers-by?

The Chamber could pass a law forcing businesses to erect tents when it rains.

Then, all of a sudden... Are you following me?... I will show you (*solemn*) the genesis of my idea... I said to myself: But why can't each citizen have his own little tent? A little piece of canvas supported by thin sticks, of bamboo for example, that you could carry yourself, over your head, to protect you from the rain.

My invention was done... All that was left was to make it practical.

This is what I imagined:

Picture to yourself a piece of cloth... silk, alpaca, whatever you like... cut into a circle, and stretched on rods made of whalebone. All of these rods are joined in the center, around a little metal ring that slides along a stick, somewhat like a cane.

When the rain stops, the rods lay against the handle, with the fabric... In that case, you can use my device as a cane.

Crack! It starts raining!... You push the little ring along the handle... the rods stretch out, and the cloth as well... You interpose this improvised shelter between you and the sky, and there you are, protected from the rain.

That's all there is to it, but you do have to think of it.

I'll bet that in three months my invention will be in everyone's hands.

You could make them in all prices, cotton for the working class, silk for the wealthy.

But it's not enough to invent something, you have to baptize your creation.

I considered words in Greek and Latin, the way they do in science. But I decided that would be pretentious.

So I said to myself: Let's see... I came up with an elegant invention, let's give it an elegant name. My device is meant to provide a little shade, so I'll call it "little shade" in Italian: umbrella.

But I'm nattering on. I'm off to the patent office; I don't

want anyone to steal my idea. Because, you know, when an idea is in the air, you can't be too careful.

Time Well Spent

In that era—now a good ten years ago; how time flies! —I paid my rent at intervals that were irregular, but none too close together.

It hasn't changed much since then, but now I have a fine landlady who contents herself with asking now and then:

"Well, M. A..., are you thinking of me?"

"Why, yes, Mme C...," I reply, with an irresistible smile, "I never stop thinking of you."

And she continues, sadly:

"It's just that I'm rather strapped at the moment."

"Not as much as I, Madame C..., not as much as I!"

In the era to which I refer, I found myself prey to a landlord who showed no scruples in scattering to the four winds of public auctions my heterogenous furniture and collections (comprising mostly stolen items).

I made up my mind, and, disgusted with the Latin Quarter, sought refuge in the first hotel I saw in the Poissonière neighborhood, perfectly unfamiliar to me, besides.

A calm and patriarchal residence, inhabited by people I never saw on the stairs, and who went to bed at unbelievably early hours of the night.

I was embarrassed.

In vain did I come home with the chickens, I was always the last to retire.

I didn't know my fellow tenants, but their shoes held no mystery for me.

By the light of my wax matches (contraband), I got to know and recognize them, and never confused them.

For example, I knew that number 7 wore big laced boots of fawn leather, while number 12 had adopted kid ankle boots with buttons.

And all these shoes, set out on their respective mats at night, seemed like so many mute reproaches.

"What?" said number 3's elastic ankle boots. "You're just coming home, and it's already dawn."

Number 14's polished shoes joined in:

"Vile debauchee, where have you been? In some low dive, probably, or someplace even worse!"

And I fled, humiliated, down the dark corridors.

A single consolation was allowed me: a mat that never insulted me.

Not that it was ever devoid of leather; on the contrary, always two pairs: one a woman's, one a man's. The woman's, pretty, minuscule, with adorably high arches, and obviously always in the service of the same feet.

The man's, variable, diverse, and never the same from one day to the next.

Sometimes, elegant boots; on other days, solid shoes with laces; or else big flat shoes, full of comfort.

But always good well-made footwear.

The men always changed, and I could tell that they were all healthy and well-to-do.

But, come to think of it, did they really change that much? Not that much, because, by force of habit, I began to recognize them and to know their usual days.

Thus, the solid shoes spent Tuesday night on the infamous mat.

Wednesday night was reserved for the fine boots, and it was always on Sunday evening that I saw the big flat shoes.

Only one day in the week, or rather one night, were the pretty little booties alone.

And how bored they looked, the poor little things!

I often thought of suggesting my company, but I didn't really know them well enough.

And regularly, every Thursday night, the little booties languished in their pitiful solitude.

I had never seen the hospitable woman, but I burned with desire to enter into relations with her; her booties were so inviting!

And one fine day, in the afternoon, I knocked at her door.

A sort of little bourgeoise, infinitely lovely, a bit too serious maybe, answered.

I was afraid I was mistaken, but a quick glance at her shoes reassured me: she was the right person.

I fired up my ships and declared my passion.

She listened to my request with a serious little expression, like any good businesswoman who receives an offer and is disappointed to refuse it:

"I'm terribly sorry, sir, but it's impossible... all my time is taken."

"Even," I insisted, "Thursday?"

She thought for two seconds.

"Thursday? I have my double amputee."

Family

Ribeyrou and Delavanne, the two inseparables, had spent Sunday afternoon in the Latin Quarter. With scrupulous conscientiousness, they had visited all the bars that had hostesses, and all the grand cafes.

Around seven o'clock, they suddenly remembered a dinner invitation on the boulevard de Clichy.

The omnibus for Place Pigalle held out its arms to them. They installed themselves, a bit moved.

The vehicle's route took it through the quai des Orfèvres.

Very curious, that quay. All the houses looked alike: shops on the ground floor, and above the shops a low little mezzanine, which seemed more like a ship's cabin than an apartment on solid land.

As the boutiques themselves are also rather low, the buses come to the same height as the mezzanine, and when they drive close to the sidewalk, you enter the apartments with astonishing ease.

That was exactly what happened with Ribeyrou and Delavanne. Slow traffic stopped their omnibus, and, for a long minute, in spite of themselves, they joined a family gathering.

It was above the boutique of a heraldic engraver.

Everyone was there together, around a table where an appetizing soup was steaming.

There was the papa, the mama, two tall young ladies, dressed alike, about twenty years old, and another little girl.

The weather was superb, that evening, and all those fine people were dining with the window open.

The bus was so close that one could smell the delicious aroma of beef stew.

Ribeyrou and Delavanne, completely bewitched by this interior tableau, already felt a sweet emotion moistening their eyelids.

The bus started off.

Delavanne broke the silence.

"That's family life."

"Ah, it must be good!" responded Ribeyrou.

"Better than the life we're leading."

"And less exhausting."

"Well, let's get off the bus. I want to see those fine people once more."

Unfortunately, on foot, they couldn't see as well. They could only get a glimpse of the circle of light the lamp made on the ceiling.

They continued on to the place Saint-Michel, had an absinthe, "their last one," and climbed again onto a departing bus.

This time, there was no traffic on the quay. The mezzanine

passed before their eyes, charming, but too quickly.

They barely had time to see the mama serving the beef. And besides, was it beef?

"Ah, family life!" Ribeyrou repeated with a heavy sigh.

"Doesn't it remind you of those Dutch interiors by... that painter, you know?..."

"Yes, I know who you mean... a Flemish painter."

"Exactly."

"Do you want to see them one more time?"

"Gladly."

And the procedure began again, not only once, but ten times, and always punctuated by an absinthe, "their last one," at the place Saint-Michel.

The conductors started to worry about their strange behavior. But since the two passengers, after all, acted like everyone else, there was nothing to say.

They boarded the bus, contemplated, left the bus, climbed onto the next one, etc.

Meanwhile, the heraldic engraver's family continued dinner without suspecting that two young men were following them with such tenderness.

After the beef came the leg of lamb, and then the green beans, and then the salad, and then the dessert.

At that moment, the weather becoming cooler, they shut the window.

One of the young ladies sat at the piano. The other sang.

From the quay, you heard nothing, but you could easily guess that the music was charming.

By dint of consuming absinthes, always "their last one," the two friends were overcome with violent emotion. They wept like little babies, literally.

"Ah, family life!"

At one moment, Delavanne seemed to make an important decision.

"Come now! It's stupid to be so unhappy. Everything can be arranged. If you like, we can go visit those people and propose to those two young ladies."

You can imagine their reception.

The heraldic engraver, stupefied at first, answered them with an extraordinarily lively allocution, in which the term "filthy drunk" appeared with regrettable frequency.

Delavanne assumed a prodigious dignity:

"Your refusal, my dear artisan, would have suffered nothing by being framed in more polite language."

"And on top of everything else," objected Ribeyrou, "we have to get back to Montmartre. Let's take the bus."

"Oh, no more buses; I'm sick of them."

The next morning, the two friends, after a tumultuous night, found themselves somewhere around the bastion of Saint-Ouen, unable to reconstruct the chain of events that had led them to such a heterodox location.

While drinking "his last" brandy and cassis, Ribeyrou

burst out laughing.

"I know what it is," exclaimed Delavanne. "You're thinking about that heraldic engraver from yesterday."

"Oh, yes, in their stateroom!"

"What do you think, eh?..."

"What chumps!"

And they went to bed.

Comfort

I don't know if you're like me, but I adore England.

I'd drop everything, even the proverbial ball, for London.

I love its bars, its music halls, its old tipsy ladies in flowered hats.

And besides, there's one true side-splitter, which alone is worth the trip: the contemplation of English "comfort."

The gentleman who started the legend of English comfort certainly had a powerful imagination. I wish I could meet him!

English comfort! Ah, let me laugh awhile, before I continue.

Besides, it's all the same to me, comfort.

When, like me, you had a severe upbringing from a Spartan father and a Lacedaemonian mother, you care little for comfort.

Are the napkins missing? I wipe my hand on my sleeve. Are the sheets no bigger than handkerchiefs? Well, I blow my nose in them, then, pirouetting on my heels, whistle some popular tune.

That's what I think of comfort, myself.

And I feel none the worse for it.

And yet, once...

(I should warn my English readers, especially the ladies, that the following story is somewhat "shocking.")

And yet, once, as I was saying, I would have preferred that London (that's what the people there call the city) were a bit more comfortable.

London, you know, is not like Paris.

In one particular sense, its Winterthur Chalets, Paris is a veritable miniature Switzerland.

It is true—ah, what a pleasure to prick the bubble of illusion—it is true that the pleasant name Winterthur Chalets is often abbreviated to its initials.

But what of it, O Helvetia?

However, more hellish than Helvetian—I pick up the thread here—was my painful condition that day.

I had drunk a great deal of ale, a fair amount of stout, and a bit of port.

I was returning to my hotel. It was around five or six in the evening.

As I turned onto Tottenham Court Road, I sorely missed... Montmartre Boulevard, for example.

Montmartre Boulevard is lined with newspaper kiosks, advertising columns, and... you understand me, Parisians.

Tottenham Court Road, although a fine street, lacks those civilized amenities; and in England, you know, it's frankly dangerous to stand too close when you read a poster.

Go into some building, and ask the concierge, you say? Innocent dreamer!

In England, no concierge. (That, for example, is comfort for you.)

What to do?

My ale, my stout, and my porter had traitorously conspired for a joint escape, and I would soon have to capitulate.

Could I temporize until Leicester Square? That was the question.

I took a few steps. A sharp pain nailed me to the spot.

For me, necessity summons invention.

I noticed a superb shop, upon whose windows shone, in letter of gold, these words: ALBERT FOX, chemist and druggist.

I'm very fond of English pharmacies, due to the extraordinary variety of objects they sell: little sponges, big sponges, neckties, garters, medium sponges, etc.

I entered, resolutely.

"Good evening, sir."

"Good evening, sir."

"Sir," I continued, in the idiom of Shakespeare, "I believe that I am diabetic."

"Oh," replied the chemist, in the same language.

"Yes, sir, and I'd like to know for sure."

"It's a simple business, sir. We just have to analyze your...

do you understand?"

"Of course I do."

Then, so that I could supply the necessary sample, he led me into a small laboratory, and handed me a glass flask topped with a comfortable funnel.

Within a few seconds, the glass flask resembled a block of topaz.

I even remember—and if I mention it, it's not to boast, for I'm the first to find it disgusting—that the flask being rather small, I had to pour some superfluous topaz into something black that was simmering on the stove.

After being assured that the analysis would be scrupulously executed, I withdrew, promising to return for the results the next day, at the same time.

"Good night, sir."

"Good evening, my friend."

The next day, at the same time, the steamer *Pétrel* was on its way to Calais, carrying in its hold a tall blond youth, who was quite distinguished and highly amused.

All the same, if I ever do develop diabetes, I'll think that the god of English chemists is exacting his revenge.

Abuse of Power

When I arrived, my dear Hélène, at the age when young men choose their careers, I hesitated for a long time between an ecclesiastical position and millinery.

I would have liked to have become a priest, especially because of confession, but, for reasons developed at length in an opuscule of mine, recently published by Gauthier-Villars, millinery continued violently to catch my eye.

So violently, that in the end I opted for that profession.

The old aunt who had raised me found a good company where I could suck the fresh milk of first principles, and, several days later, I was engaged, as a young clerk, by Pinaud and Love, rue Richelieu.

The Pinaud and Love Company was then composed, as the name implies, of a man named Pinaud and a man named Love.

My new bosses immediately became my friends.

The fact is that I had everything going for me: advantageous appearance, affable manners, keen aptitude for business, conversation, ingenious observations, sparkling wit, and (which didn't hurt), relative honesty, somewhat.

In addition, I was a musician, gifted with a mezzo-soprano voice of irresistible charm.

And let's not forget, since we're at this chapter, and even though the subject is only indirectly pertinent, my uncommon aptitude for the physical and natural sciences.

Pinaud and Love seemed enchanted with their new recruit, and treated me with overwhelming consideration.

In short, everything was going as swimmingly as a fish, when July 14th arrived.

I don't know if you've noticed, but on July 14th there are many little public dances installed on the streets and crossroads of Paris.

I don't know why I say "little dances," since there are also big ones, which was the case for the one held, that year, on the place de la Bourse.

The store closed at noon, and the bosses gave their employees the day off.

My God, milords, what spirit, what bravery!

Oh, the waists abandoned to arms of steel!

Oh, the tender vows murmured between people who had only met that morning!

July 14th! Be forever blessed, holy date, for you've saved a lot of time for lovers, and for others too.

I will long remember that it was on that day that I met the first two journalists of my life.

I refer to M. Mermeix, then editor of the *Gaulois*, and to M. Mayer-Lévy (an Israelite, I believe).

These lively festivities were nearly spoiled by a regrettable accident: a small boy, trying to grab the cymbals, climbed onto the musicians' platform. His foot slipped, and there was the little fellow on the floor.

Unfortunately, the cymbals slipped as well, and gave the imprudent youth a rather large bump on the head.

While they carried him off to a pharmacist, a young woman asked me:

"What happened?"

"Oh, nothing," I said.

And, parodying a familiar verse from our national poet, I added facetiously:

The little boy received the cymbals on his head.

Without a trace of emotion, without hesitation, the young lady replied in the same spirit:

He was too fond of cymbals, and that's what caused his death.

I admired such wit and composure in a frail young lady (she was frail), and vowed at that moment my most ardent flame.

(Don't frown like that, Hélène, at this old memory. You know very well that I love no one but you. Besides, you'll see from what follows that my relations with the young lady remained almost entirely ineffective.)

The frail young lady (did I mention that she was frail?) was named Prudence.

She informed me unreservedly that I met her general standards, and we were the best of friends.

Well into the wee hours, and after dancing like lost souls, I saw Prudence home to her mother.

But she had my address, and, a thousand times a day, passed before my store.

Me, I was very happy, very happy.

The following Sunday, it was understood, Prudence would surrender to my flame.

But on that famous following Sunday, just as I was leaving, wearing my most beautiful tie, my second boss, M. Love, asked me:

"Where are you going, Emile?"

"But... I'm going out."

"You're not going out."

"Yes I am!"

"No, you're not going out, there's work to do."

"Yes I am!"

And M. Love seized me and pushed me into the back of the store.

At that time, I hadn't yet acquired the prodigious strength that has made me the Terror of Clichy-Levallois.

Seething with rage, I struggled, but M. Love held me in an iron grip.

Meanwhile, Prudence ran off with God knows who, for I never saw her again.

Love, Love, when you take ahold of us, we can only say: Goodbye, Prudence!

Extra Stories

The Two Hydropathes

(Prankish story in two tableaux, one of which is a prologue.)

PROLOGUE

It was a Saturday, at the Coucou Cafe... It must have been nine in the evening. Two young men, whom one could recognize as Hydropathes, without giving much thought to the matter, finished a mazagran generously diluted with cognac. One of them said: "It must be time to leave for the show," and, drawing a silver disc from his gusset, tapped the marble table with it. It must have been a signal, for Elise, who was sitting nearby, came to collect his money. The young man, like any good Hydropathe, left the young woman a copious tip, and both men arose.

The first put on a long ulster and a little gray hat of soft felt. The other enveloped his personality in an ample macfarlane, and topped the ensemble with an opera hat.

They left, went down the rue de Vaugirard, turned left at the boulevard Michel. At the corner of the rue Soufflot, the Ulster said:

"Let's take the rue Soufflot, the place du Panthéon, the

rue Clovis, the rue Cardinal-Lemoine, it's much quicker."

The Macfarlane answered firmly:

"You're crazy. Look. It's infinitely more reasonable to go down the boulevard Michel, and to take the rue des Écoles until the rue Jussieu."

The discussion lasted a few moments, friendly, but animated.

"I'll tell you what," the Ulster concluded. "You go by your rue des Écoles, and I'll go by the rue Clovis. We'll see who gets there first."

Both, after taking a few steps in their respective directions, returned to their point of departure, and the Macfarlane said in a defiant voice:

"And no cab, you know!"

"Don't be stupid..."

End of the prologue

SECOND TABLEAU

About eight minutes after the events we have just recounted, two hackneys violently clinked glasses at the corner of the rues de Jussieu and Cardinal-Lemoine. One had come down the rue de Panthéon, the other from the rue des Écoles.

From these two cabs suddenly emerged two young men who seemed livid with rage. The first wore a long ulster and a little gray hat of soft felt. The other was enveloped in an ample macfarlane, the ensemble topped with an opera hat.

I approached to get a better look...

It wasn't them.

End of the second tableau

Spectral Love

She was certainly dead, and probably for a long time.

By what miracle of equilibrium could she still sit upright, on her high chair, behind the counter in the brasserie?

How could she still move, that dead cashier, and how could she, at every moment, respond to the waiters and to the customers?

Force of habit, probably, and a faint impetus left over from her past life.

When she was alive, she must have worked for a long time as a cashier, for, despite her premature demise (she must have died when she was thirty), she still had a prodigious sureness of hand, and singular ease in the handling of tokens and carafes.

Her skin was pale, with greenish tints that sometimes reflected the amber of the cognac bottles, and the piles of sugar cubes, on the counter before her.

Her hair, ashen and abundant, had that shriveled look one sees in dead women's hair.

Sometimes, with especially friendly customers, she seemed to forget the sadness of her situation, and she smiled.

Then her wan lips opened, showing teeth that were very

beautiful, very white, very straight, but teeth of the dead, like dull dry ivory.

Her eyes had retained vague glimmers that saddened you, when you felt them on you, and her hands, so long and white, hurt you just to look at them.

In what padded coffin, on what funeral bier did she sleep, at night, after closing?

By what miraculous antiseptics had she achieved such complete conservation?

For a long time I asked myself these questions, and very gradually I felt my heart grow tender toward the poor deceased, who had never found the rest she had the right to expect.

She noticed one day, and wanted to abandon with me that supreme indifference that death usually gives.

Then one fine night, after the little mutual game of glances and furtive words (she was closely watched by her boss), she placed her fleshless arm on my arm and we left together.

To stay until closing, I had to drink a great deal. Furthermore, the strangeness of the situation intoxicated me further, but with a macabre and troubling tipsiness.

The words and music of my friend Rollinat ran through my head.

She spoke to me in her slow sweet voice, somewhat low for a young woman, but still charming.

Once in the room, I was somewhat afraid, and, while she undressed, I closed my eyes.

In my turn, I got into bed.

The touch of her cold thin body made me shiver.

Then there was a rush, never interrupted, of mad kisses, tortuous caresses, passionate embraces.

The touch of my dead companion, the sepulchral timbre of her voice, the gas lamp whose pale green light reflected to infinity in two parallel mirrors, everything contributed to terrify me.

Not a minute of respite punctuated the drunkenness of that bizarre night.

Suddenly, she pulled herself from my arms, opened the curtains wide, and blew out the melancholy lamp.

The sun was shining.

O miracle! O transformation!

She seemed dazzlingly pink and alive.

Very thin, but with the charming thinness of adolescence, she stood before me, smiling sweetly.

She must have been about seventeen.

Me, not believing my eyes, I gazed stupidly at her, without realizing her delicious transformation.

She understood my mute astonishment, and, approaching the bed, placed two long tender kisses on my eyes, saying in a low voice:

"I got so much rest!..."

The Spirit of Ellen

That night, I had returned home weary and agitated. It had been a year since Ellen was no more, and for the first time I had been untrue to her memory. On her deathbed, she had made me swear to stay eternally faithful. I, mad with grief at the idea of that terrifying separation, knowing that once she was dead, all would be finished for me, I had promised what she had asked, with her last poor agonized smile.

Until that day, I had never broken my vow; my cult for Ellen's memory had remained religious and exclusive.

And then one day, in a riotous outing, led by joyous companions and beautiful women, I had forgotten everything. My friends, hoping to rid me of what they called my depression, had conspired to get me drunk, and to throw me into the arms of some hussy.

Their plan was successful. The woman was superb, quite buxom but still young, with a red fleshy mouth, and big bulging eyes, the eyes of a grazing cow.

The image of my dear departed never left me, but so vague, so blurred in the distant blue of my memory, that I was not too cruelly obsessed with her.

The copious wine, the women's aromas and perfumes,

had awakened the beast in me, that brutal and filthy beast who, long dormant within, was finally compensated.

And then, in the morning, disgust welled up in me, melancholy and irremediable. Shame at my weakness made me flee the woman so suddenly that she suspected a fit of madness. All day, I walked feverishly, trying to forget my disgrace. In vain.

Always before me arose the pale phantom of Ellen, whose expression of cruel reproach drove me to tears. With the evening, my anxiety became more terrible and more precise. I dared not return home, so sure was I of seeing the woman I had betrayed.

So, when I finally entered my apartment, I was less surprised than frightened.

Ellen was there, her back to me, in the chair before my desk. As far as I could tell in the dim light, she wore the white dressing gown she used to put on when she could still leave the bed.

In the room floated her favorite perfume, a heavy and troubling scent dominated by wintergreen, which her sisters had sent from America, and which she preferred to any other.

I halted at the threshold, mute with terror. My courage returned, and, knowing full well that I was prey to a hallucination, I struck a match and stepped forward.

There was in fact, no one in the chair. Nothing had been

disturbed. But how had the perfume spread throughout the room?

That scent that she adored had always been odious to me, and I had needed all my love and patience to tolerate it.

Furthermore, I had packed all her toilet articles in boxes, and had never touched them since her death, so much did the sight of them revive my grief.

I opened the windows and walked out onto the balcony, until the scent had completely dissipated, then my fatigue overwhelmed my anxiety, and I fell asleep.

Not for long. A quick soft noise, like the nibbling of a mouse, had started. From time to time, it was punctuated with a sharp and rapid knock. The same perfume began to float through the room more intensely than before.

I struck another match and looked. Nothing abnormal in the room. As long as the match burned, I heard nothing, but as soon as it went out the faint sound began again. Then, sometimes, paper rustling.

Listening carefully, I determined the nature of the sound: someone was writing in the room.

This time, I lit a candle and got out of bed. Again the noise stopped. Everything seemed in order on my desk. Trying to laugh at my own imagination, I returned to bed. As soon as it was dark again, the fantastic pen continued racing across the paper, stopping only to get more ink.

Mad with fear, I hardly dared move beneath the covers. Then I either passed out or simply fell asleep, but I don't remember when the noise stopped.

I slept heavily until late in the morning. When I awoke, I remembered everything, and naturally attributed my nocturnal hallucinations to a nightmare.

What was my terror, when, driven by a curiosity that I thought unnecessary, I went to examine my desk.

The ink bottle, which I always keep carefully stoppered, was open. A pen lay there, still wet with fresh ink. A sheet of blotting paper had been taken out and used, assuredly not by me, since I only use powder.

The blotter had obviously been used on a fresh page. The last lines and the signature were clearly visible, but unreadable, because of the reversal. The idea of using the mirror to restore the writing came naturally to me.

At once I saw the signature "Ellen," horribly clear. It was her usual handwriting, but with something cruel and precise about it that chilled me. No matter how I tried, I could read nothing else, for the page, blotted after it had dried, had left only blurred traces.

Since that moment, I have never enjoyed a moment of sleep. Every night, a strange perfume, dominated by wintergreen, fills my apartment.

Desperately, I keep trying to read in the mirror the illegible flyspecks, and all rest is gone forever, for

Ellen will never forgive my contemptible betrayal.

Christmas Story

It was three years ago, that is, at Christmas time, that I found myself locked in a little prison in Yorkshire, convicted of theft, swindling, and blackmail, along with a rather nasty morals charge, on which it would pain me to linger.

What vexed me the most about my situation was less the imprisonment itself, than the time at which it occurred.

I've always adored Christmas, that holiday of children and the hearth, Christmas, good old Christmas.

Mistletoe, mistletoe, still more mistletoe!

In England more than anywhere else, and particularly in Yorkshire, the Christmas season has an intimate character, which the traditional Parisian sausage evokes only faintly... so faintly...

As for intimacy, I had no complaints. My cell was quite intimate, maybe even too much so.

My jailer had me... Oh, what a strange jailer! He was a former horse-guard, who had lost a leg in the war against the Ashanti.

Since he had originally enlisted in the horse-guards for the uniform, he had insisted, despite his amputation and his new job, in keeping his former outfit.

And it was truly comical, to see on one side a wooden leg, and on the other a leather pants leg, a boot, and a spur.

Very comical and very touching!

Meanwhile, despite all of these details, Christmas Eve had arrived.

And I who was invited to a party in the Faroe Islands, with the holy family of an evangelical pastor!

All of you who read this, or almost all of you, have been in prison; but, when in prison, have you seen it snow?

Oh, what a horror, the snow that falls when you're in prison!

The only sensation that connects you to the world outside, sound, sweet noise, disappears.

You see nothing, you hear nothing!

And it fell without stopping, at a slant, thick, dense, so much that my poor little cell was dimmed and smothered with it.

I missed one sound the most, among those I had noticed and loved since my captivity: that of my jailer walking in the prison courtyard.

First, *bang*!... the dull impact of the wooden leg on the pavement, and then the triumphant and victorious *toc*!... of the boot, metallized by the jingling of the spur, one after the other.

Was my old horse-guard no longer walking, or were his steps muffled by the snow?

I asked myself these questions with that vain anxiety fostered by the idleness of cellular life.

Christmas Eve had come, and I still couldn't decide to go to bed.

The bells rang in the city first, then in the little neighboring parishes.

Those last, muted by the snow, veiled by distance, and so moving that I felt my eyes grow wet.

I've always wept when I heard, in the distance, the country church bells.

"Come in!" I said, waking from my reverie.

Someone had just knocked on the door of my cell.

It was a little pink and white girl of about fifteen, carrying on her left arm a little basket, and holding in her right hand a thick bunch of mistletoe.

"Good evening, sir," she said.

"Good evening, miss," I replied.

And she continued, still in English:

"Don't you recognize me?"

"Of course," I replied in the same language. "I think I met you once in a book by Kate Greenaway."

"No, not there."

"Then, in a beautiful picture by Robert Caldecott."

"Not there, either."

A moment of silence.

"What?" she asked, with a mischievous smile. "Don't

you remember? Last year, you saved me from certain death. I was crossing Trafalgar Square, when, prey to a sudden and violent rage, one of the bronze lions there pounced on me. I barely had time to escape. An omnibus passed by, with you on the upper deck. You leaned over, and with one vigorous arm lifted me from the voracity of the beast. Sulking, the animal resumed its immutable position, and the decorative role to which the artist had assigned it."

I consulted my memories in vain, but could recall nothing analogous. But she insisted:

"It was the Bull and Gate omnibus. You were going to visit your friend Lombardi, in the Villa Chiavenna."

Before such a precise fact, I could only bow.

She produced from her basket the plum pudding of recognition, along with several bottles of ale, and we dined joyfully.

At dawn, she disappeared, taking my heart and the empty bottles.

Since then, I have tried to remember that curious incident in Trafalgar Square.

I never could.

It's true that I also have no memory of the prison in Yorkshire, the jailer with the wooden leg, the pink and white girl, the plum pudding, or the bottles of ale.

It's funny, in our existence, how we forget everything.

Widow's Son

At 256 rue Rougemont, in an apartment two floors above the mezzanine (three thousand and five, plus taxes), lived a family called the Martin family.

This family was composed of three people: a father, a mother, and a son.

The father, at the moment in which this story begins, had just retired from business.

Founder and director of the "General Insurance Agency Against Notaries," he had made an immense fortune in this enterprise.

A tranquil man, unsociable even, and in that the exact opposite of his wife and son, he cordially detested society parties, balls, and theaters.

His wife and son, forgetting all courtesy, called him a cross old bear.

Mme Martin had counted more than thirty springs, but she was not yet ready for the fortieth.

Pretty, elegant, and frivolous, everyone thought she was her husband's daughter and her son's older sister.

Her son, a nice boy of eighteen, abominably spoiled by his mama, a bit wild, already borrowed relatively considerable sums from his father's friends, from the grocers, and even, once, from the concierge.

A mother's heart holds cartloads of indulgence. Mme Martin paid it all back, without telling her husband.

One day, the younger Martin committed an escapade so scandalous that it could not be hidden from his father.

The father mounted his highest horse, fulminated, and decided that Gaston would immediately enlist for five years.

A mother's eyes are eternal and spacious reservoirs of tears. Mme Martin shed torrents.

All in vain; M. Martin was stone.

The only concession he made to the weeping mother was to let her accompany the child to the door of the barracks.

At the moment of separation, the orderly sergeant, moved by her sobs, suggested that Mme Martin go see the captain and the colonel to recommend her son.

The unfortunate woman began with the captain, a young captain of thirty, a healthy young buck.

She stayed for a quarter of an hour, and left somewhat comforted.

Then it was the colonel's turn.

As it happened, the colonel was very gradually approaching sixty.

Mme Martin's visit lasted around three quarters of an hour.

But she left completely comforted.

Not for long, for Gaston's first letters were disturbing.

They had eaten all his chocolate.

And then there was a distressing picture of military life: bad bed, dirty food, nasty comrades, painful duties, rough exercises, bullying, blanket-tossing, etc.

The only good moment in the week was when, on Sunday afternoon, the regiment band played the *Flowerpot*, the prestigious polka-march by Willy (Henry Gauthier-Villars, Reserve Second Lieutenant).

Mme Martin, one fine day, could take no more.

She took a train and visited the colonel.

The colonel had not aged, but was no younger, either.

After three quarters of an hour of supplication, he finally let himself be moved, and, against all regulations, granted second class soldier Martin a week's leave.

The next day, a family dinner reunited the three members of the Martin family.

The father was less inexorable, on this occasion.

But it was about time!...

Before heading for bed, as was his immemorial custom, M. Martin leaned against the balcony and lit his pipe, his good old pipe.

The mother and son chatted in the morning room.

"So," said the mother, "you say there's no way to get out of that awful regiment?"

"None, mama, unless I'm declared unfit for service, or become a widow's son..."

"A widow's son, you say?"

"Yes, mama, a widow's son."

The mother thought for a moment, then asked suddenly:

"Are you particularly attached to your father?"

"Not at all, mama, and you?"

"Oh, me!..."

And she made a gesture expressing perfect disdain for her spouse. Then she continued:

"Well, watch this."

At that moment, M. Martin was leaning far over the balcony.

His center of gravity was not beyond the balcony, but it wasn't far.

It was obvious that the slightest displacement of his mass toward the street must result first in a loss of balance, and then in a fall.

Mme Martin approached on tiptoe, seized the cuffs of her husband's trousers, and poof! sent him to meet, by the most direct route, the object on the sidewalk he had been studying so attentively.

This movement was executed with a vigor and precision one might not expect in a woman of such fashionable appearance.

When M. Martin, his fall completed, struck the asphalt,

it made a *plmmf*, the flat and muffled sound of meat hitting the pan, and, at almost the same time, *teck*, the sound of his meerschaum pipe breaking.

M. Martin had indeed "broken his pipe."

A young woman who was passing by, leaving the theater, found herself splattered with gray specks.

As she began to wipe her dress with her handkerchief, an obliging passerby told her:

"That's brain, madame, it won't stain. Let it dry, and tomorrow, after a good scrubbing with a brush, it won't even show."

The passerby was wrong; the human brain contains fat (phosphorated), and stains cloth like any other fatty substance.

Meanwhile, Mme Martin and her son raced down the stairs.

"My husband, my poor husband!' sobbed the wife.

"Papa, my poor papa!" shouted the son.

And the crowd was moved, respectfully uncovering before this immense and double sorrow.

A fat and wheezing doctor ran up to them.

He certified the death, and took their names and address to collect his little fee the next day.

The funeral of M. Martin was quite a beautiful funeral.

Dressed in mourning, with a black armband, racked by convulsive sobs, the young Martin led the service.

"Poor boy," said the crowd.

There was a brief judicial inquiry which attributed M. Martin's death to a fall caused by an apoplectic attack.

The widow's son returned to civil life, to the great despair of the colonel, who was quite fond of Mme Martin.

Despite my keen sympathy for the widow and orphan, I will not conceal the fact that the period of mourning was somewhat abbreviated.

Sooner than one might have decently expected, they reappeared in society.

Some people would waltz on the banks of the Styx.

But here's the funniest part of the whole story:

Mme Martin, with her son's consent, plans to remarry.

They didn't realize, that frivolous pair, that Gaston, after his mother's marriage, would no longer be a widow's son, and would be recalled.

I, as you might guess, have no intention of telling them.

And I'm highly amused in advance, at poor Gaston's face.

The Enchanted Forest

"A superb night!" cried Wilfrid, returning from the garden. "What if we went back on foot?"

It was around nine o'clock. We had dined copiously at a farm in the middle of the woods, about ten kilometers from town.

"On foot?" I asked, with a grimace of relative enthusiasm.

"Why yes, of course, on foot! If you're tired, I can carry you."

The idea of this nocturnal and sylvan promenade seemed so appealing to my friend Wilfrid that I agreed to it.

Our host launched into meticulous directions for the shortest way home (which, in the woods, is never a straight line).

I lent fervent ears to the unraveling of this webwork, but Wilfred, the big idiot, said:

"Yes, yes, I get it, first left and then right... Yes, we'll find it easily."

We found it so easily that, after an hour, neither of us knew where we were.

To add to our misfortune, dark clouds gathered, monstrous flocks of them, as if deliberately hiding the chlorotic Phoebe.

Began the mutual recriminations:

"You see," I said, "if we'd taken a cab back, we'd be home, at this time of the night, instead of wandering lost in the great forest, like Hop-o'-My-Thumb."

"If you're a cripple," Wilfrid acrimoniously replied, "you should stay at home."

"And when you have as bad a sense of direction as you, you should bring along signposts..."

"To slam you in the face with, if you say another word."

(Wilfrid wouldn't flick a Spanish fly, but he affects violence in his language.)

During this time, we wandered down a path that was as poetic as anything, but where the most desperate human couldn't have hung himself from a lamppost.

Suddenly, Wilfrid cried:

"Over there... A light!"

It was true. At the end of the path, a vague brightness filtered through the branches.

We quickened our pace.

As we advanced, I became concerned. What would we find when we arrived?

Tall white houses with balconies, immense gilded signs rose up before us. A pharmacy sparkled, dazzling with polychromatic bottles, an immense Parisian cafe spread out a thousand tables and chairs.

And then a cab station, billboards, newspaper kiosks, innumerable streetlights. Paris, in a word!

I asked Wilfrid to pinch me, to wake me up.

Wilfrid invited me to provide him with a few grains of hellebore, to dissipate his hallucination.

Can you imagine our situation? In the middle of the forest, some fifty leagues from Paris, at night, and we stumble across a stretch of the boulevard Montmartre!

And we were both awake, neither of us mad.

We arrive; our feet step upon the asphalt sidewalk.

Nobody in the street, nobody in the shops, nobody at the windows.

Just four old men, smoking their pipes and drinking beer, on the terrace of the cafe.

Without understanding exactly what danger threatens us, Wilfrid and I are vaguely disturbed.

We sit at a table in the cafe and order drinks. A waiter, very correct, serves us with the most natural air in the world.

At that moment, one of the customers seems to take pity on our confusion.

"These gentlemen," he says, "seem surprised to find themselves in the middle of Paris at this hour?"

We confessed our surprise.

"It's quite a story," the man continued. "I'll tell it to you. I was born in Paris in a building on the boulevard, I was an apprentice barber in a building on the boulevard, a barber in a building on the boulevard, a shop owner on the boulevard. I never left the boulevard, it's where I made my fortune. To live without the boulevard, without its kiosks, its streetlights, its shops, its cab stations, is impossible for me... Last year, I fell seriously ill, and my doctor prescribed the air of the forest. How bored I was, in that forest, far from my boulevard. So, I decided to build a little stretch of boulevard, with its accessories, in a piece of forest I'd bought... These gentlemen you see, who look like generals, lawyers, and businessmen, are simple woodcutters, whose hair and beards I've cut to look like Parisian society. You can make fun of me, but it's all I need to make me happy."

We didn't make fun of him, quite the contrary; because a man who can make himself happy with a simple illusion is infinitely wiser than one who is miserable with reality.

A Stroke Of Luck

A true stroke of luck for the *Chat Noir* and its readers. Everyone was surprised by the sudden interruption of the *Maxims* published recently in the *Echo de Paris*, maxims from the powerful brain and prestigious pen of M. Alexandre Dumas.

This sudden interruption was energetically discussed in literary milieus, and even in several diplomatic circles. Many high echelons were deeply alarmed by it.

The time has come to explain the enigma: the *Echo de Paris* will no longer publish M. Dumas's *Maxims*, because the *Chat Noir* has acquired the exclusive rights.

For their weight in gold, we might add, for the administration, which never shrinks before any sacrifice, did not hesitate to offer the celebrated dramatist on the avenue de Villiers ten centimes more (per maxim) than he was paid at the Colbert Hotel.

Presented with this sudden and unexpected counterbid, the grandson of Alexandre Dumas's father blanched, tottered, and capitulated.

He put only one condition on the deal:

"Sign them," he implored, "with a pseudonym opaque enough that I won't be recognized."

"Trust us," replied the administration.

And that is how today we can begin the publication of the Maxims by... But shh! We promised not to tell.

Let's go:

Maxims

First Seventeen

I

God acted wisely in placing birth before death; otherwise, what would we know of life?

II

How many people, today, would agree to live in the glass house of the virtuous? What about frosted glass?

III

What is more inhuman than human sacrifice?

IV

One good thing about poverty is that it decreases the fear of thieves.

V

I have known many *filles de joie* whose fathers were men of sorrow.

VI

It has been said that genius is an act of patience. And marriage, then!

VII

Married men age more quickly than bachelors; it's like the drop of water that, falling constantly on the same place, finally wears out the hardest granite.

VIII

Statistics have shown that mortality in the army augments appreciatively in times of war.

IX

Some lighthouses are shaped like candles. They also have the same illuminating power, in the same proportion, of course.

X

God made no blue food. He wanted to keep azure for the firmament and the eyes of certain women.

XI

A beautiful stupid women who is well dressed is like a beautiful empty bottle with a superb label.

XII

To do an act of charity is good. To make other people do it is better.

That way, you help your neighbor without troubling yourself.

XIII

Neglecting payment has caused... the rupture of many ephemeral couples.

XIV

The ticking of clocks is like mice nibbling time.

XV

To marry a cocotte is to paint your number on the side of a bus.

XVI

Police are wrong to mistreat criminals. Without them, they wouldn't exist.

XVII

In the winter, the poor gather dead wood in the countryside. Dead wood is better than green, because there is no fuel like an old fuel.

DUMAPHIS

Translator's Notes

"A Philosopher" (*Un philosophe*): January 4, 1890.

Tranquille comme Baptiste ("as calm as Baptiste") is an expression that apparently surfaced in the early 19th century. Its origin is uncertain: it either refers to a character in 19th century farces, an actor in 18th century farces, or John the Baptist. Whoever he was, he was tranquil.

"Ferdinand": February 1, 1890.

Belvaux is a town in Luxembourg; however, *bel veau* means "beautiful fool," which may be more germane here.

Datura stramonium is commonly known as jimson weed, Devil's snare, thornapple, moon flower, hell's belle, devil's snare, devil's trumpet, devil's weed, devil's cucumber, locoweed, stinkweed, or pricklyburr, and can be quite toxic.

"Customs of the Times" (*Moeurs de ce temps-ci*): Apparently, previously unpublished.

Parisian bartenders reckoned the bill by the number of saucers a customer had accumulated.

"On the Town" (*En bordée*): November 14, 1885. Its original title was *Canon en goguette* ("Cannon on a Spree"); it was revised for the book.

Montcocasse might well be heard as *mon cocasse*: my funny fellow.

"As Good a Way as Any" (*Un moyen comme un autre*): February 28, 1885. In the *Chat Noir*, this dialogue was subtitled "A story for Guy Cros (six years old)." Guy was the son of Allais's friend and collaborator Charles Cros.

"Collage": October 31, 1885. The story was entirely rewritten for the book. Among other changes, Dr. Snowdrop was originally named William K.

There is, in fact, a Pigtown, in Carroll County, Ohio. The story "Esthetic" also takes place in this quintessential American community.

"Little Pigs" (*Les petits cochons*): September 7, 1889.

Andouilly is not on the maps; an *andouille* is literally a sausage, and figuratively an idiot.

Alfred Capus was a journalist, novelist, and playwright, In 1896, he collaborated with Allais on a play, *Innocent*, which Allais later reworked into his novel *The Blaireau Affair*.

"Cruel Enigma" (*Cruelle énigme*): February 11, 1888.

The little room described in the first few paragraphs is taken from Victor Hugo's poem *Souvenir de la nuit du quatre* ("Memory of the Night of the Fourth") in *Les Châtiments* (*The Punishments*) from 1853, in which a boy is killed (with two bullets, not three) in the coup d'état that installed Napoleon III as emperor.

"The Doctor" (*Le médecin*): December 15, 1888.

"Boisflambard": March 15, 1890.
Boisflambard means "burning wood," but *flambard* has the added meaning of "braggart."

"No Consistency in His Ideas" (*Pas de suite dans les idées*): November 6, 1886.

"The Height of Darwinism" (*Le comble du darwinisme*): May 19, 1888. Originally dedicated to Lionel Nunès, a lawyer who was Pissarro's cousin and a friend of Renoir's.

Fleurant is the apothecary in Molière's *Imaginary Invalid*; Marin Feynarou killed his wife's lover, Louis Aubert, in 1882.

Madame Benoîton was a character in Victorien Sardou's 1865 play *La Famille Benoîton*; she never appears, since she's always out doing something else.

Jacques-Bénigne Bossuet (1627-1704) and François Fénelon (1651-1715) were bishops and theologians.

"Taupin's mines" was a joke that Allais used several times. There is no such place as Taupin; however *mine de houille à Taupin* recalls the old expression *sec comme les couilles à Taupin* (as dry as Taupin's balls). The origin of the phrase, and the identity of the unfortunate Taupin, are unknown.

"To Set His Mind at Ease" (*Pour en avoir le coeur net*): February 14, 1885.

"The Palm Tree" (*Le Palmier*): November 2, 1889.

"The Circumspect Criminal" (*Le criminel précautionneux*): March 7, 1885.

This short tale was based on one of Allais's *combles*, which first appeared in *Le Tintamarre*, October 28, 1877: "The height of cynicism: To murder a shopkeeper during the night, and to paste on the storefront: Closed because of death!"

"The Kisser" (*L'embrasseur*): July 26, 1890.

N. Hervé de Lumièges is a pun on the famous painting by Évariste-Vital Luminais, *Les Énervés de Lumiège* (1880), depicting the two sons of the seventh century king Clovis II, their tendons cut, cast adrift.

I suspect Simili-Meyer is Arthur Meyer, the editor of the conservative *Gaulois*. Meyer opened the first wax museum in Paris (hence the "Simili"), and sported impressive muttonchops (hence the beauty mark).

"The Benevolent Suicide" (*Le pendu bienvaillant*): May 16, 1885.

A piece of rope from a hanged man was considered good luck, particularly if given by the man who cut down the corpse.

"Esthetic": July 7, 1888, as *Un Salon en Amérique*.

The epigraph is in English in the original. Sir Cordon Sonnett's name is eerily reminiscent of *cordon à sonnette*, "bell rope."

The Gallery of Machines was a popular attraction at the Universal Exposition in 1889.

Blagsmith will inevitably call to mind the word *blague*, "joke."

George-Ern. Baker was apparently fictional.

"A Thoroughly Parisian Drama" (*Un drame bien parisien*): April 26, 1890, but dated April 1.

This has become one of Allais's most popular stories, having been chosen by André Breton for his *Anthology of Black Humor*, analyzed in great detail by Umberto Eco in his book *Lector in Fabula*, as well as inaugurating Black Scat Books in an illustrated adaptation by Norman Conquest (*Masks*, Absurdist Texts & Documents Series #1, 2012).

The quotation from Rabelais comes from Book Four, Chapter VII. It's Dindenault's response when Panurge buys a sheep, the very sheep that will soon lead the rest into the sea, followed by Dindenault. Peter Anthony Motteux translated it as "Ah! How well the knave could choose him out a ram!"

Henry d'Erville was a regular at the Chat Noir, nicknamed "The Colonel" for his distinguished appearance and military bearing.

The epigraph for Chapter II also served as the epigraph for Chapter 15 of Stendhal's *Le Rouge et le noir*. It may have been written by Stendhal. However, it also shows up as the epigraph to *Les Deux Fous*, by Paul Lacroix, also from 1830, so maybe Lacroix wrote it. At any rate, it doesn't seem to actually date from the Renaissance, despite its old spelling. In the *Chat Noir* version, it was attributed to Darwin.

The Théâtre d'Application was a popular theater from 1888 to 1909. *L'Infidèle*, by Georges de Porto-Riche, did indeed play there in 1890. It was published that year by Paul Ollendorff, which lists Marguerite Moreno as Vanina, but Albert Laroche as Lazzaro, and Kraus as Venato. Étienne Grosclaude was a journalist, not an actor, and, I suspect, would have been miscast in the role.

"Hold your tongue, please!" is in English in the text.

The Incoherents' Ball, an outgrowth of the Incoherents' Exhibits organized by Jules Lévy, took place from 1885 to 1891.

Auguste Marin (1860-1904) was one of the chief

member of the "Marseille school" of poetry. Much of his poetry, like the couplet Allais quotes, was in Provençal.

Le Diable boiteux was a daily paper that ran from 1823 to 1825, and was revived briefly in 1848 and 1857. Its full title was *The Limping Devil, Journal of Theater, Manners, and Literature in 19th Century France*. It was named after a 1707 novel by Alain-René Lesage.

Henry O'Mercier seems to be resolutely imaginary. His name, though, could be heard as *on rit au mercier*, "One laughs at the haberdasher."

George Auriol was another Chat Noir regular, and a good friend of Allais's. A poet and songwriter, he became best known as a graphic designer; one of his Art Nouveau typefaces was used for the Paris Metro. The epigraph comes from a show he wrote with Narcisse Lebeau, *Pourvu qu'on rigole!* (*As Long as We Laugh!*). Allais, writing as Sarcey, gave it a good review in the *Chat Noir* (Dec. 20, 1890), and also quoted the full quatrain:

Buvons le vermouth grenadine,
Espoir de nos vieux bataillons.
Celui qui dort, celui-là dine!
Buvons, buvons, buvons!

Let's drink vermouth with grenadine,
The hope of our old battalions.

The one who sleeps, is the one who eats!
Let's drink, let's drink, let's drink!

"Mam'zelle Miss": March 14, 1885.

"The Good Painter" (*Le bon peintre*): January 17, 1885. Originally dedicated to Luigi Loir, a painter active in Paris at the time.

"The Zebras" (*Les zèbres*): November 9, 1889.

Arthur Sapeck, born Eugène Bataille, was a caricaturist, composer, singer, poet, ventriloquist, and above all, practical joker. He participated in the Hydropathes, Hirsutes, Fumistes, and Incohérents. Allais called him "the emperor of pranksters." After increasing bouts of mental illness, he was committed to the asylum of Clermont sur Oise in 1889, and died there in 1891.

Villerville and Trouville are near Honfleur, Allais's hometown; Sapeck seems to have invented Grailly-sur-Toucque.

Mère Toutain's inn on the Saint-Siméon Farm was a favorite of artists, including Gustave Courbet, Eugène Boudin, and Claude Monet.

"Simple Misunderstanding" (*Simple malentendu*): March 29, 1890.

This little tale was later expanded into the play *Silvérie, or the Dutch Fund*, written with Tristan Bernard, and inflated even further into the ghost written novel *Le Boomerang*.

The Gotha is the Almanach de Saxe Gotha, the directory of European nobility; the Bottin is the French phone book.

Fluctuat nec mergitur, "tossed by the waves, but not sunk," is still the motto of Paris.

Deyk-Lister's unusual name may suggest *des clystères*, "enemas."

"The Young Lady and the Old Pig" (*La jeune fille et le vieux cochon*): August 21, 1886.

The original version had a footnote attached to the penultimate line: "It is a widespread superstition, in certain parts of the Auge valley, to bury the cadavers of dead pigs in fields of colza." Colza, or rapeseed, is not only grown for its oil, but as fodder for pigs.

"Sancta Simplicitas": July 6, 1889.

"Sancta simplicitas," "holy innocence," is reputed to be Jan Hus's reaction to an old woman he saw gathering the wood to burn him at the stake.

"A Really Good One" (*Une bien bonne*): June 1, 1889.

A *rigouillard* is a joker.

"Dirty Trick" (*Truc Canaille*): September 28, 1889.

The Pactolus was a river on the Aegean coast, in what is now Turkey, known for containing gold dust. According to legend, it was where Midas washed off his golden touch, and where Croesus acquired his wealth.

Pierre-Joseph Proudhon was, for those rusty on their anarchy, the coiner of that phrase.

"Anesthetic" (*Anesthésie*): May 10, 1890.

Lecoq-Hue is, appropriately, *le cocu*, "the cuckold."

"Irony" (*Ironie*): March 7, 1885.

"Tickets": March 8, 1890.

Tout au poil means "everything's fine."

"A Little 'Turn of the Century'" (*Un petit "fin de siècle"*): February 15, 1890.

"Inflame the Bacchante" (*Allumons la bacchante*): January 29, 1887.

Gustave Boulanger was indeed a member of the Institute, and particularly known for his paintings of women.

"Fancy Dress" (*Tenue de fantaisie*): November 30, 1889.

Lemballeur is an *emballeur*: literally, a packager; in

slang, a cop.

"Aphasia" (*Aphasie*): June 15, 1889.
Val-de-Grâce is a military hospital in Paris.

"A Bizarre Death" (*Une mort bizarre*): November 10, 1888; dedicated to Jean Richepin, poet, playwright, and novelist.
Auguste Rispal was City Councillor of le Havre at the time.

"Mockery Punished" (*Le railleur puni*): January 1, 1887.
The footnote refers to a kerfuffle with Léon Fourneau, aka Léon Xanrof (*fornax*, Latin for *fourneau*, backwards) who had published a very similar story in the *Courrier Français*, on February 8, 1891. Fourneau protested that it was an old story his grandfather had told him; Allais suggested that perhaps a thief could explain that the watch he'd stolen was his grandfather's.
Potinbourg-sur-Bec doesn't seem to be strictly geographical; it might be rendered as Gossipburg-on-Mouth. The Marché des Veaux is the calf market, probably keeping in mind that *veau* also means "fool." Hume-Mabrize means "smell my breeze."
Although Maurice Éguisier is credited with inventing an improved enema, there's some doubt that the credit

should be entirely his.

Yvette Guilbert was a star of the Moulin Rouge, and a favorite subject for painters.

"Oddities" (*Excentric's*): June 30, 1888.

Francisque Sarcey was a theater critic, the butt of Allais's persistent ridicule.

"The Calf" (*Le veau*): December 20, 1884.

Sara was the daughter of Rodolphe Salis, proprietor of the Chat Noir.

"Traveling" (*En voyage*): September 22, 1888.

Jacques Amyot translated Longus's *Daphnis and Chloe* in 1559.

Must I explain who Buffon is? What has the world come to? Just in case: Georges-Louis Leclerc, comte de Buffon, was an important naturalist. His *Histoire naturelle*, in 36 volumes, was long a standard reference.

"The Tumultoscope" (*Le chambardoscope*): January 31, 1891.

The duke shows up in some of Allais's other stories; unfortunately, his name sounds like *du conneau de la lunerie*, "of the idiot of foolishness."

Appropriately, Laflemme's name means "laziness."

"We are not cattle" (*On n'est pas des boeufs*) became the title of Allais's seventh collection.

Mazas Prison was a prison in Paris from 1841 to 1900.

Émile Richebourg wrote popular novels and serials, especially for the *Petit Journal*.

"An Invention" (*Une invention*): June 12, 1886.

In the *Almanach illustré du Père Ubu* (Alfred Jarry, 1901), Ubu also invents the umbrella after being caught in the rain on the rue de Rivoli. Homage? Plagiarism? Coincidence?

"Time Well Spent" (*Le temps bien employé*): November 13, 1886.

"Family" (*Famille*): May 1, 1886.

Well, Ribérou is a port town, and a *vanne* is a floodgate; I don't know if that helps.

"Comfort": January 7, 1888.

"Abuse of Power" (*Abus de pouvoir*): August 4, 1888.

Gauthier-Villars was a publishing house specializing in scientific literature. Henry Gauthier-Villars, the son of its director, led a colorful career as a writer and critic under the name of Willy, and is now best remembered as Colette's troublesome husband. He also conducted a memorable feud with Erik Satie.

Pinaud and Amour was indeed a hat shop in Paris.

Gabriel Terrail, known as Mermeix, was a socialist and a journalist, influenced successively by Blanqui and Boulanger. He had nothing to do with the conservative *Gaulois*. Its editor, Arthur Meyer (already invoked in "The Kisser") was indeed Jewish, the son of a rabbi, but opposed Dreyfus, fought a duel with Édouard Drumont (who had accused him of being Jewish), and eventually converted to Catholicism.

The first line of Victor Hugo is from *Souvenir de la nuit du quatre* (alluded to above, in "Cruel Enigma"): *L'enfant avait reçu deux balles dans la tête*, "The child had received two bullets in his head." The second line, also by Hugo, is from the poem *Fantômes*, in *Les Orientales* (1829): *Elle aimait trop le bal, c'est ce qui l'a tuée*, "She loved dancing too much, that's what killed her."

EXTRA STORIES

"The Two Hydropathes" (*Les deux Hydropathes*): This precursor to "A Thoroughly Parisian Drama" appeared in *L'Hydropathe*, March 15, 1880, and was then reprinted in the *Chat Noir*, January 9, 1886.

The Hydropathes were founded in 1878 by Émile Goudeau, and included Allais, Sapeck, and Charles Cros, among others. The name could mean either "those who cure by water" or "those who shun water"; the members tended to the latter interpretation, and met to enjoy poetry, pranks, and alcohol. "Goudeau," it was often remarked, sounded like *goût d'eau*, "taste of water."

"Spectral Love" (*Amour spectral*): February 21, 1885.

Maurice Rollinat often recited and sang his verses at the Chat Noir. His 1883 collection *Les Névroses* (The Neuroses), was influenced, one could even say excessively, by Poe and Baudelaire.

"The Spirit of Ellen" (*L'esprit d'Ellen*): April 25, 1885.

"Christmas Story" (*Conte de Noël*): December 26, 1885.

Kate Greenaway and Robert Caldecott were both English illustrators, especially of children's books.

Chiavenna is, in fact, a town in Lombardy, far from Trafalgar Square.

"Widow's Son" (*Fils de veuve*): October 1, 1887.

Henry Gauthier Villars wrote under the name of Willy, although usually prose, not polkas. In 1887, however, he did publish a *polka-marche* for piano, *Pot de Fleurs,* which he further embellished with the initials "H. G. V. S. L. D. R.": Henry Gauthier-Villars, Sous-Lieutenant de Réserve. I should add that he often used ghostwriters, including his wife Colette, so that it's likely he didn't write the piece himself. Allais used the initials without explanation, which meant a bit of research for his translator.

"The Enchanted Forest" (*La fôret enchantée*): October 27, 1888.

"A Stroke of Luck" (*Une bonne fortune*): January 11, 1890.

Allais used this premise to trot out some of his favorite one-liners, many of which appear elsewhere in his stories.

"Dumaphis" is transparently *Dumas fils,* the son of Dumas.

ABOUT THE TRANSLATOR

Doug Skinner has contributed to *Black Scat Review, Oulipo Pornobongo, The Fortean Times, Strange Attractor Journal, Fate, Weirdo, The Anomalist, Nickelodeon, Cabinet,* and other fine publications. His books include *The Unknown Adjective* (picture stories), *Horoscrapes* (altered horoscopes), *Sleepytime Cemetery* (short stories), and *The Doug Skinner Dossier* (short works in many genres).

His translations include *Three Dreams* (Giovanni Battista Nazari, Magnum Opus Hermetic Sourceworks, 2002), *Merde à la Belle Époque* (various, Black Scat, 2012), and *The Zombie of Great Peru* (Pierre-Corneille Blessebois, Black Scat, 2015). Black Scat has also published several of his translations of Alphonse Allais.

He has written music for several dance companies, including ODC-San Francisco and Margaret Jenkins, and for actor/clown Bill Irwin (*The Regard of Flight, The Courtroom,* and *The Harlequin Studies*). TV and movie appearances include *Great Performances, Martin Mull's Talent Takes a Holiday, Ed, Crocodile Dundee II,* and a smattering of commercials.

He was long active in Manhattan, singing his songs in clubs, doing puppet shows with veteran performance artist Michael Smith, and projecting his cartoons on the wall. He has recently moved to New Paltz, a few miles to the north.

This illustrated chapbook is a darkly humorous, pataphysical tale – celebrated by André Breton and the Surrealists, and hailed by the Oulipo. Allais's clever paradox is a prime example of Jarry's inspired "science of imaginary solutions." Illustrated throughout by Norman Conquest, *Masks* includes a most Allaisian introduction and notes on the text by Doug Skinner.

Perfect-bound in full color. 50 pages. *Absurdist Texts & Documents* No. 1.

"The first and last anarchist in France." — Rachilde

The Squadron's Umbrella collects 39 of Allais's funniest stories — many originally published in the legendary paper *Le Chat Noir,* written for the Bohemians of Montmartre. Included are such classic pranks on the reader as "The Templars" (in which the plot becomes secondary to remembering the hero's name) and "Like the Others" (in which a lover's attempts to emulate his rivals lead to fatal but inevitable results.) These tales have amused and inspired generations, and now English readers can enjoy the master absurdist at his best. As the author promises, this book contains no umbrella and the subject of squadrons is "not even broached."

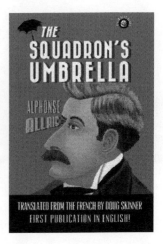

Allais's only novel, *L'Affaire Blaireau,* has been adapted to film four times and has remained popular and in print in France since its original appearance in 1899. This is its first publication in English. and features—in the words of translator Doug Skinner—"Summer in the provinces, the shrewd but impressionable Blaireau, futile political squabbles, a ridiculous but charming love story... and innocence is rewarded!"

"...effervescent and flavorful, perfect in its way." –*Wuthering Expectations*

The Alphonse Allais Collection
published by Black Scat Books

---•◦•◦•---

"... one of the great masterpieces of humorous literature."
—nooSFere Littérature

"...apart from being long-awaited, *Captain Cap* also comes at a timely moment because its ironies are particularly apposite today as we witness global intellectual colonization." *— Leonardo Reviews*

Translated and with an introduction, notes, and illustrations by Doug Skinner, this is the complete, unabridged text of the original 1902 French classic by the peerless humorist, Alphonse Allais. This deluxe edition also features eight uncollected "Captain Cap" stories, plus a "Cappendix" of rare historical pictures. Over 360 pages of absurdist mirth and howls of laughter.

*"Allais comes across as a very modern writer, and his work as an experimental enterprise which is exemplary in many ways... it is also quite possible to invoke such writers as Queneau, Calvino, and Borges." —*Jean-Marie Defays

This collection of Allais's rare theatrical texts includes original translations—never before published in English—of ten monologues, three one-act plays, and twelve shorter dialogues, skits and burlesques drawn from his columns in such publications as *Le Chat Noir* and *L'Hydropathe*. This delightful compilation by Doug Skinner (with fascinating notes on the texts) is proto-Dada at its most delicious.

"No Oulipian could fail to be enchanted by his essentially ironic tales, in which he juggles the rhetorical and narrative components of writing with rigorous logic and inexhaustibly zany results."
— Harry Mathews

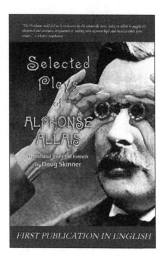

Made in the USA
Columbia, SC
02 March 2025

54604493R00167